In Loving Memory

John L. Ulrich, M.D.
and
A.M. Powell

Listen
to the
Whispers

Published by Dobson Powell Press
18550 West Outer Drive
Dearborn, Michigan 48128
dobsonpowellpress@gmail.com

For information regarding sales and fulfillment:
sales@annarbormediagroup.com

Book design and layout by Words Plus Design, www.wordsplusdesign.com

Printed in the United States of America

First Edition
ISBN 978-0-9672436-1-0

Contents

Acknowledgments

This book reflects the dedication of many people. I am grateful, beyond measure, to each one of you:

Marcy Waldinger, my wife, whose love, devotion, and unwavering support have made my dream a reality;

Jason and Emily, my children, who are, beyond expression, the greatest joys of my life;

Rebecca Powell Waldinger, my mother, whose unconditional love and remarkable insight are treasured;

Richard Waldinger, my father, who instilled within me the belief that I could accomplish whatever my heart embraced;

Amy Lax, my sister, who gave me the greatest gift a brother can have — a sister who will always be there for me, always with love;

Martha Ulrich, thank you for being a blessing in my life; the book began when I met you and Dr. Ulrich;

Don and Bette Mys, whose commitment, enthusiasm, and keen intellects have been invaluable to me for the past twelve years. Cherished lifelong friendships were formed; Bette also introduced my poetry to Stevie Wonder and a collaboration was born. The poems "Nature's Tap Dance," "A Dream Come True," "Together Again," and "I Begin As I End" are dedicated to Stevie Wonder;

Jan Smith, whose gentle spirit and kindness were always appreciated, journeyed with me through the creation of *Listen to the Whispers*; no challenge was too great for her to undertake;

Alice Nigoghosian, Associate Director, Wayne State University Press, retired, who graciously offered to share her experience in the midst of an extremely busy schedule;

Mary Sharon Joseph, whose editorial talent was of enormous help;

Jim Edwards, Carl Allore, and Lee Lewis Walsh, whose expertise and counsel in publishing, editing, and formatting were invaluable in the production of this book;

A special thank you to my current and former staff for their efforts on my behalf: Andi Goward, Beverly Miller, Linda Konfara, Loretta Burke, Sheila Kaniewski, Suzi Habhab, Teresa Kujat, Lisa Sherman, Ernestine Maycock, Bertha Denhard, Phyllis Preston, Pansy Combs, Eleanore Tauriainen, Shirley Smith, Daisy McCune, Verlene Wells, Sharon Martin, Sherry Fuhrman, Marcia Wheeler, Joan Sall, Christine Russell, Kathy Becker, Danielle Bozvi, Leslee Beszka, Elaine Chrapkiewicz, Sherry Ossy, Lisa Rusnak, Brenda Hannah-Bergman, Debra Taft, Nicole Woodruff, and Joanne Beasley.

I am especially grateful to my patients who so generously and unsparingly shared their stories. You are an inspiration each day.

✑

Foreword

It is my privilege and pleasure to introduce Thomas Waldinger's book, *Listen to the Whispers*. In 1997 he talked with me at his office about contributing to his book. I was profoundly moved by his mission to honor the memory of his mentor by sharing the philosophies of his patients that reflect their wisdom, their values, their faith. We have worked together almost every day for twelve years and have become great friends. In part, the book is a result of the special relationships Dr. Waldinger has formed with his patients. He appreciates the uniqueness of each person in a kind and gentle way. His poetry is a window to his soul and is a wealth of beauty, love and faith.

The sentiments and wisdom expressed in this book have been a major influence in my life. One of Dr. Waldinger's patients, Sister Therese Mary, writes, "A book such as yours stimulates self-examination regarding what really matters and is invaluable. Your writing is of particular beauty to me as both a professional and a religious. I share your values regarding the place of God as First Love and Source of Strength."

My professional career was as a teacher/consultant for the visually impaired. When I was a student teacher in 1960 at The Michigan School for the Blind in East Lansing, one of my students was Stevie Wonder. In addition to student teaching, I resided and worked in the school dormitory and I was Stevie Wonder's dormitory mother. Our friendship began in 1960 and we have remained friends ever since. The world knows Stevie Wonder for his music and commitment to social justice. I know him as a remarkable, kind, loving soul.

Stevie Wonder has mentioned to me over the years that he would like to do one special thing for me to honor our friendship. In the course of our forty-nine-year friendship I have had only one request: to make songs from Dr. Waldinger's poems. Twelve years ago, when I read the poems to Stevie Wonder, he felt a connection to them and began to create songs using Dr. Waldinger's poems as lyrics.

I am grateful that in my life's journey I was able to form a bridge between Stevie Wonder and Tom Waldinger — two kindred souls. They have both been a blessing in my life.

— Bette Mys, Editor

Listen to the
to the
Whispers

Introduction

This book was written to honor the memory of John L. Ulrich, M.D. Dr. Ulrich had the most profound effect on my adult and professional life.

In 1984, I was completing the final year of my dermatology residency at the University of Michigan Medical Center and interviewing across the country to determine where to establish my practice, when I learned that Dr. Ulrich was seeking an associate.

In October I had the opportunity to meet with Dr. Ulrich. I felt a tremendous warmth, caring, and spiritual quality from him. I remember his smile and pleasant voice. Dr. Ulrich gave me a tour of the office and then we sat in an examination room to talk. I couldn't help but notice that the mural in the exam room — a country scene with a meadow, pond, trees, and a waterwheel — was the same wallpaper as in the dining room of my home. At the end of our first meeting, Dr. Ulrich looked at me in his kind, compassionate way and said, "God bless you and your family." This was the person I wanted to join in practice.

There was one other defining moment in my life. In 1974, my sophomore year of college, while studying in the dormitory library and absorbed in a chemistry book, I looked up and noticed a friend coming to say hello. She was accompanied by a woman I had never seen before. I knew immediately, even before we were introduced, that this was the person I wanted to marry. This was particularly striking since I was concentrating on my pre-medical studies and marriage was the furthest thing from my mind. Our mutual friend introduced Marcy and me that day in the library. We were married in 1977 and this past June celebrated our thirty-first anniversary.

These two events changed the course of my life.

On July 1, 1985, I began practicing dermatology with Dr. Ulrich. I noticed he had a most remarkable connection with each of his patients. He believed that if you truly love and care for your patients and do everything medically possible for them, God will take care of the rest. Although Dr. Ulrich was thirty-five years my senior and from a different era, we shared the same vision and professional philosophy. I had truly met a kindred spirit. We worked together Mondays and Wednesdays for five years, sharing a small office with only three exam rooms. We brought our lunch from home and ate together in our office.

Upon leaving the office in the evening, Dr. Ulrich's parting words were, "God bless you." He always shared the same special warmth and caring with me that he extended to his patients. His sincerity had great meaning for me. I was always able to speak with Dr. Ulrich about all of my concerns. He would listen carefully, offer his advice, but always emphasize "give it to the Lord." During my first several months of working with Dr. Ulrich, he would not accept payment for assisting me with patient care because he said I needed "time to get on my feet." This is another example of the generosity and thoughtfulness of this very special person.

One Saturday of a Labor Day weekend, a patient called me at home needing dermatological care in the office. Since Dr. Ulrich's home was nearby, I suggested that Marcy and my daughter, Emily, accompany me to visit Dr. and Mrs. Ulrich. Dr. Ulrich had made me feel like a member of his family and encouraged me to visit anytime. I wanted Marcy and Emily to hear Dr. Ulrich's life story, which he had shared with me during our lunches together.

After seeing my patient, we went to Dr. Ulrich's home. Dr. and Mrs. Ulrich were delighted to see us. We visited for several hours while Marcy and Emily listened attentively to Dr. Ulrich's fascinating life story. Although I had heard these stories during our lunchtimes, I enjoyed hearing them again, as if for the first time. When I spoke with Dr. Ulrich the following week, I told him how much we enjoyed spending time with him and Mrs. Ulrich.

Several weeks after the visit, Mrs. Ulrich called to tell me that Dr. Ulrich had been admitted to the hospital. That evening I went to be with him. He wasn't able to speak, to see or hear me. I felt fortunate that we had spent so much time together and that he knew how much he meant to me. Dr. Ulrich passed away on November 11, 1997 at the age of eighty-two. I often recall the Labor Day weekend my patient called me, grateful that my family had shared that evening with the Ulriches.

For quite some time after Dr. Ulrich's death, I felt a deep sadness and sense of loss. I regretted that I did not have a permanent written remembrance from him. Although we had spoken about his faith and approach to life and I did possess personal letters from him, nevertheless, I wished that I had asked him to write his life story and include seminal moments and events that he had not shared with me before. I felt certain that I would have learned even more from his written thoughts and that they would have guided me, as he had, for years to come.

Because my patients bestowed much kindness and warmth upon me, I was reminded of my close bond with Dr. Ulrich. I realized that I could learn from my older patients by requesting their written philosophies. This was the very opportunity that I had missed with my great friend. My patients had shared their thoughts, their joys, their hardships with me. Their written philosophies would be a heartfelt tribute to Dr. Ulrich's memory.

Dr. and Mrs. Ulrich share special time with Emily Waldinger, May 1989

In seeking the philosophies of my patients, I learned more about Dr. Ulrich and about myself. Although I had great fulfillment from medicine and excellent rapport with my patients, I noticed that my relationship with the patients who shared their life experiences with me transcended the typical doctor-patient interaction. Not only was I learning from my patients in ways I could not have anticipated, but I had greater joy as a physician and in my personal life. I will be forever grateful to my very kind and thoughtful patients for sharing so much of themselves.

⤝

Always On My Shoulder

You showed me the way
From dust to breath
From dawn to dusk
You showed me the way.

If I had wings
I would fly
Rest on the clouds
Search every star
To tell you
Deep in my heart
You will always be
You showed me the way
Always on my shoulder.

Renewal of spring
Warmth of summer
Color of autumn
Snow of winter is falling
The symphony of seasons
Always on my shoulder.

Leaves appear on the trees
Swans settle on the lake
Lake run rainbow swim upstream
Swallows fly south
The symphony of seasons
Always on my shoulder.

So this is where I am
Settled in my soul
Every day I remember
Memories are forever.

If I had wings
I would fly
Rest on the clouds
Search every star
To tell you
Deep in my heart
You will always be
You showed me the way
Always on my shoulder.

— Thomas P. Waldinger

The Impossible Takes
a Couple of Minutes

At the conclusion of each day at my office, I carefully review the charts of all scheduled patients. My office staff writes a note on the chart if a patient was unable to come so that I am notified of the reason for the cancellation.

One evening, as I was going through this daily ritual, I read that one of my patients had been seriously injured in a plane crash. I called his home and spoke with his wife. She told me that he was critically injured and in a coma. Over the course of the next year, I called this gentleman's family to see how he was progressing. His recovery was protracted and difficult.

Approximately one year after the accident, I saw this patient in my office. He was partially paralyzed, had short-term memory loss, and had difficulty speaking. Nevertheless, he was extremely happy to see me. To my astonishment, he displayed the same robust smile and positive attitude that he possessed prior to the accident.

He returned periodically in the ensuing months for additional medical treatment. Again, at each visit, I noticed that his cheerful spirit was no different than it had been from the first day we had met. I thought to myself that his significant and challenging medical problems had not changed his spiritual essence. This was certainly a most remarkable and courageous person. As we sat in the exam room, I wondered how he was able to maintain his heroic and positive attitude in the face of such adversity.

Because he had always displayed such warmth toward me, I felt comfortable asking him the following question: "It is amazing to me that after all that you have been through, you still have an optimistic attitude and warm smile. How are you able to do this?" He looked at me, smiled, and said, "Doc, I was a Marine. The difficult we do right away. The impossible takes a couple of minutes."

From that moment, I gained greater insight into his positive attitude. This was a person I had always enjoyed, but now, I had learned something unique about him. I continued to think about this individual throughout the day and into the evening; I realized that a question that I was hesitant to ask opened the door to his soul.

When I initially spoke with the older patients who contributed to this book, I asked them to share their thoughts based on this question: "If you had one hour left to live, what would you say to your children or grandchildren?" As I read their stories, I recalled the inspiring moment when my patient said, "The difficult we do right away. The impossible takes a couple of minutes." The process of seeking the wisdom of my patients facilitated a connection with their spiritual essence. I began to realize that the spiritual essence and the wisdom of a person can be reflections of each other. When you seek one, you will find the other. The wisdom of a person can be life-transforming; the spiritual essence of a person can be life-comforting.

In several cases, my patients focused on experiences in their lives that they had never shared with anyone — their spouse, a friend, or a relative. Although these patients never intended to hide a part of their lives, it was the actual process of writing their philosophies of life that caused self-examination and self-inquiry and resulted in sharing previously untold memories. Writing one's philosophy creates a new self-awareness and clarity that affords the potential for resolution of personal difficulties and shared struggles. The conversations that result from this search can be a reservoir of warmth, love, and knowledge.

One of my patients, Mrs. Bette Mys, was working on her own book when I asked her to share her thoughts with me. Bette stopped working on her project and offered to be my editor — a beautiful sentiment, a gift of friendship. One day in December 1998, we were having lunch in my office, working on my first book, *The Wisdom of Life Through My Patients,* when Bette suggested that I write a poem to include in this book. I remember thinking that it would be both meaningful and the fulfillment of a lifelong desire to continue writing poetry. This became the genesis for *Listen to the Whispers.*

Writing poetry expresses my philosophy of life. I dream and stretch my soul. I pray for peace. I pray that people will see beauty in our differences. I look at the wonders of creation and hope that as we share the human experience, we recognize that faith and love are one.

Listen To The Whispers

You are the reason
You are my rainbow
You are a dream
Each moment is precious.

Like a blue moon
Twice my love
Beauty and grace
My heaven on earth.

Sit by my side
Hold my hand
In the stillness
In the silence
There is great wisdom.

Listen to the whispers
They are sent from above
Listen to the whispers
The greatest of these is love.

When you are tired and weary
Rest your head on my shoulder.
Lift your eyes to the heavens above
The greatest of these is love.

Embracing you
I found myself
Like a blue moon
Twice my love

Always have time
To tell you
I love you
I love you.

Look back to learn
Look forward with you
My heart is yours forever
Listen to the whispers
Listen to the whispers.

Sit by my side
Hold my hand
In the stillness
In the silence
I am with you always.
I am with you always.

Listen to the whispers
They are sent from above
Listen to the whispers
The greatest of these is love.

— Thomas P. Waldinger

Part One

The Gift from My Patients

No one person has all the world's wisdom.
People everywhere share small pieces
whenever they share ideas.

— Ashanti folk tale

Mr. John Griffin

*"As I grow older, I am trying to learn what really matters in life.
I fail most of the time, but at least I get up and try again to really
learn that love and acceptance of everyone and every day and
every experience are what really count."*

I'm seventy-three years old, a widower, father of ten children, and grandfather of seventeen. I'm an adjunct professor of psychology at the University of Detroit-Mercy and, in addition, the executive secretary of a tool and die manufacturers association. I'm in love with reading (more nonfiction now), and partially addicted to that most frustrating of all activities, golf — or, to be more correct, my peculiar version of the game.

In my seventy-three years, my strongest memories are of the magnificent dignity that my wife, Ann, showed while suffering the erosion of her body and mind to Alzheimer's disease. Second, I also recall the courage displayed by my best friend and assistant squad leader, Carl Steinle, who was killed in action in Germany in 1945. In seven months of combat, he was the only man I ever saw who showed no fear in combat.

As I grow older, I have tried to learn what really matters in life. I fail most of the time, but at least I get up and try again to really learn that love and acceptance of everyone and every day and every experience are what really count. Tolstoy's *Where Love Is, There Is God* and

Death of Ivan Ilyitch teach me these truths each time I read these stories.

Now, two stories about Ann Griffin, my wife. She hadn't spoken for two to three years — not a single word. Our son, Pat, who lived in San Francisco at the time, came to visit her. A few of us were in the room. The nurse said, "Look who has come to see you. Do you know him?" Ann said, "Yes. That's my son, Pat."

My second story about Ann was that four years later, after four years of complete silence, four years of my visits three times a day, seven days a week, four years of talking and holding her and tending to her, four years of loving her even more than all of the years before, she looked at me as she often looked at me. Out of deep spools of confusion and a heaping-on of heavy layers of forgetfulness of a long-buried life of blankness, somehow these words fought through — the last words she ever spoke — only three words: "I love you." She was a magnificent woman.

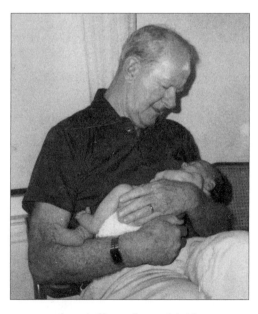

Mr. John Griffin and grandchild, 1994

When Love Is Shared

We share the human experience
The search for meaning in our lives
The joy of love and friendship
The response to hardships and tragedy
The revelation of faith.

The sadness of loss of a loved one
The hope and dreams for a newborn child
The responsibility for our thoughts and actions
The quest for knowledge and renewal.

For so long
I struggled with myself
Could not see
All God's beauty
Could not rest
With tranquility
Could not understand
Lack of unity.

There is great peace
Trusting
In the Divine
There is great humility
Believing
In a Supreme Being
There is great love
Sharing
My life with you.

We share the human experience
There is an elegance
A romance
A radiance
To life
When love is shared
When love is shared.

— Thomas P. Waldinger

Mrs. Wanda Haywood

"I pray that my grandchildren will always remember that the good will outweigh the bad and apply it to their lives. I pray that God will keep them in His protective care and when I have to leave here, they will know I am still with them, through my love for them."

I was born in a mining camp in a place called Green Castle in the rolling hills of West Virginia. Born Wanda Lee Jenkins, August 16, 1938, to a couple by the name of Gladys Faye (Tincher) Jenkins and Marion Sam Jenkins.

I was born in the mountains where you can stand and look over the valleys and see the rivers running for miles with streams of water flowing from the mountains. I remember snow-capped trees in winter and a picture postcard of colorful hues in the fall.

I sometimes go home on what is called Bridge Day on the New River Bridge at Fayetteville, West Virginia, where the bridge spans the river from one mountain to another. It is the longest single-arch bridge in the world and people come from all over the world to parachute off the bridge on that particular day.

My father, needless to say, was a coal miner. He started to work, crawling and digging his way through the mines, at the age of nine. He was a hardworking man and a very good father. Every time we heard the whistle blow at the mines, we knew someone was in trouble. As a rule, that meant a cave-in or a fire. My dad was given up twice for dead

Mrs. Wanda Haywood's parents, 1965

from cave-ins, but God had other plans and spared his life, for which we were very thankful. My mother was a wonderful mother. She took very good care of us. I have five sisters — Katherine Marie, Emmogene, Marleen, Drema Ruth, and Veronica Lynn. God called my dad home in 1980 and my mom in 1986.

I used to spend many hours in the company store where they eventually made the movie *Matewan*. My dad worked for the coal company that owned this store. We would walk five miles to get scrip to buy food and goods from the store. Most of our food was homegrown or raised. My dad raised chickens and hogs and grew a garden. Our hams were hung to cure and we made our sausage and baked pork rinds. We also made our own lye soap.

I also remember when times were so bad that we would share a skillet of water gravy with the family from across the railroad tracks. Our Christmas tree was always cut fresh, because they were always plentiful. We made what we could to decorate, but we never bought any decorations. Our stringing of popcorn was always fun. I walked miles to and from school in grades one through five. I shared with other students a one-room schoolhouse where our teacher would cook a pot of beans while she taught us and the potbelly stove warmed us. This same teacher had taught our mother what education she had, which was not too many years, as she was married at the age of fourteen. My dad was a self-taught man who knew a little of everything.

Our life was a hard one, but a good one. I remember a very strict home that was always full of love and a lot of good times. We had an icebox and sometimes a truck would come by and we would buy a block of ice. That was a treat to have something cold for a change. We also studied our homework by an old oil lamp. We had to carry our water from a spring or the pump we had to prime. We also caught rainwater to wash clothes and scrub the floors. We would use this same water to wash our hair, to make it softer. We carried our coal and chopped our wood for our fireplace. There was no gas heat or electricity, at least not in our part of the country. We had an outhouse, as there was no indoor bathroom. We also had Saturday night baths in the big tub. We had a creek that ran behind our house, so we washed often.

Our dad would shovel a path from our house to the outhouse and the snow was so deep you would be afraid the snow would fall in and bury you alive. We had this footbridge that we called a swinging bridge. That was a good name for it, because it really did swing.

My mother washed clothes in a tub and on an old washboard. I saw her small hands bleed many a time as she did this and hung our clothes out to dry. She would stand and press them with an iron she had to heat on the old coal stove. I wonder now how she could have held so much love in her heart for all of us.

We used to string beans and hang them up to dry. They were called leather britches. We fixed these to be eaten in the wintertime. We picked blackberries and made cobblers, jams, and jellies. I still do these things every now and then, with the exception that I pay more attention to the snakes now than the berries.

On the Fourth of July, the company store would deliver a case of pop and two gallons of ice cream packed in dry ice. Our games were marbles and kick the can. We also did this silly dance called the May pole dance.

I never knew either one of my grandfathers because they had passed on before I was born. I had two wonderful grandmothers. I still think of my mom's mother and how I used to go out in the yard and pick apples from the trees, sit under the beechnut tree for hours, and run through the field of flowers. My mom would bake sweetbread that had an aroma that would make your mouth water. We would make snow ice cream, and listen to a radio that was powered by a car battery. I listened to "Boston Blackie," "The Squeaking Door," and "The Grand Old Opry."

I often think of my mother, especially when I design a ballet costume for my granddaughters. I remember my mother's talents in the area of arts and crafts and how she encouraged me to follow in her footsteps. She used to make our clothes from the feedsacks she would save until she had enough of the same pattern. Or, we could order from the catalog, or buy from the old peddler who came by twice a year. I sure can relate to Loretta Lynn's song, "The Coal Miner's Daughter," for I have been there. I sure had a lot of dreams when I was young, but a lot less money. Somehow the love replaced the money, and I have had a wonderful life.

At the age of sixteen, I met and married a wonderful man who was nineteen. He had gone into the Marines at the age of sixteen and had just gotten out. His name is Frank Haywood. He has been a hard worker, a good provider, and loved me even when I couldn't love myself. Most of all, he has always been my good friend. He was stricken with colon cancer in 1995, and hope was dim. By his faith and God's loving grace, he has extended our wonderful life to date.

We thank God daily for His many blessings. Frank and I thought, what is a missing colon and the rest that went with it. As long as we can have quality life and be together, we will take it and be forever grateful.

I love reading and teaching Sunday school to teenage girls. Frank and I also play a little music and sing. We have one son, Frank Haywood, Jr. He designs houses and teaches college, works as an inspector, and is in construction development. But most of all he is a wonderful father to our precious granddaughters, Hillary Caitlin and

Haley Lauren Haywood, and a good husband to our daughter-in-law, Julie. We thank God so much for them. Hillary and Haley have been the reasons for us to go on when we felt that we could not. We are very proud of our son and have an undying love for him, and thank him so much for our granddaughters.

I have enjoyed tracing our family roots. I searched for years and one day went to the Burton Historical Archive in Detroit and there found our family's book on a shelf. What a thrill when I saw my mom and dad's names there, and to know there were a lot of important people I was connected to. I pray that my grandchildren will always remember that the good will outweigh the bad and apply it to their lives. I pray that God will keep them in His protective care and when I have to leave here, they will know I am still with them, through my love for them.

Soon I will celebrate my sixtieth birthday. My mind wanders back to a time in my life as a young girl when my five sisters and I endured a life of poverty, as did many others. The only difference was the love we had to replace the poverty, which made me a stronger person. Our mother was very strict, but always gave us the love we needed and her prayers have gone a long way. She always taught us to give love and kindness to our fellow man and it would always be returned to us.

This brings me to a very special man, Dr. Thomas Waldinger. I recall the first time I met him. I wondered if this doctor could be for real. I could feel a genuine concern and a love that had to be God-given. I remember when he told me that I had cancer on my nose. The earthly part of me was afraid, for I had recently lost my father to cancer, but the spiritual part of me was at peace. Dr. Waldinger told me he could operate on me in the office or, if I wanted, he could send me to the hospital to have it done. I told him to operate on me in his office, for I trusted him and had faith in him and in God. I felt God had everything in control. I felt at that time, and still do to this day, that Dr. Waldinger is a precious soul that God leads daily.

Three years ago, my husband was stricken with severe colon cancer that had spread and the prognosis was not good. But thanks be to God, he is still here and enjoying our precious granddaughters, Hillary and Haley. Also, we have four other children whose lives God has allowed us to share — Jennifer, Kassie, Andrew, and Josh. We are not legally their grandparents, but our hearts say they are ours.

Always With Love

I can talk with you all night
We can help each other
Like no other
Because I believe in you
And you believe in me.

Awake to the autumn air
Walk with me
Trees become rainbows
Miracles all around
Listen to nature's sounds
Beautiful birds sing
None compares to you
Miracles all around
Listen to nature's sounds.

My renaissance
Your essence
No coincidence
God's presence
Because I believe in you
And you believe in me.

I can talk with you all night
We can help each other
Like no other
Miracles all around
Because I believe in you
And you believe in me

Always with love
With love always
Miracles all around
Always with love
With love always.

— Thomas P. Waldinger

Mrs. Margaret Reilly

"My Uncle Lee . . . reminds me of Dr. Ulrich; both were tall, handsome, kind, and gentle. Every time Uncle Lee and I parted, he said, 'Sugar, if you need anything at all, just call me.' Dr. Ulrich's parting words were, 'Bless you.'"

It is important that I start these remarks by saying that my sister and I are a mixture of Northern "Yankee" (so called by my mother's family) and a soft, gentle Southern woman. My father was born into a prominent, prosperous Michigan farm family, who enjoyed a warm, wonderful life with an abiding faith in God and in education. His parents' dream for their three sons was that someday they would attend college and earn engineering degrees. When my dad was eight years old, his mother died, and then four years later, his father was killed in a car accident. Eventually the inheritance disappeared and the boys were placed in a Chicago orphanage. The youngest boy stayed in the institution and graduated from high school, the middle boy ran away, and the oldest boy, my dad, stayed until sometime during high school and then returned to Michigan to fish and to be with his brother.

When Dad was in his early twenties, he went to Ford Motor Company's Rouge manufacturing complex in search of a job. At five in the morning, applicants formed a line outside the employment office. After the candidates were chosen for the jobs that day, a Ford personnel employee approached Dad and said, "If you had not been standing with your hands in your pockets, you would have gotten a job today." Needless to say, at five the next morning, Dad was back in line, standing with his arms straight down at his sides. He was hired that day and worked at Ford Motor Company for forty-three years. It was not uncommon for Henry Ford to look over Dad's shoulders, watching him work. Dad attended Henry Ford Trade School, worked on experimental projects, such as automatic transmissions, and received Ford Motor Company's highest monetary award for the invention (one among a number of others he was too humble to claim) of cost-saving machinery. Dad was a very bright, dedicated, loyal employee, often working seven days a week for months on end, absent one day for the birth of a daughter (my sister) and late one morning because of car trouble. Without question, Dad possessed an exemplary work ethic, a product of the Great Depression that impressed upon him a set of rules for the rest of his life, ethics conferred upon his daughters — no doubt about it.

Dad believed education guaranteed a means to earn a decent living and a way to keep you out of long employment lines. Education is exactly what he wanted for his daughters. My sister graduated from a California university with a Bachelor of Science in Business and subsequently earned her C.P.A. She began her professional career as the first woman auditor in Los Angeles for Arthur Andersen and Company, one of the largest accounting firms in the world. She went on to become vice-president of finance for a southern California hospital and medical center. I earned a Bachelor of Science and a Master of Arts in Business and taught in secondary schools for over thirty years.

I am proud to report that, from both sides of the family, we have seventeen first cousins, eleven of whom are college graduates — accountants, engineers, lawyers, teachers, a world-class scientist, a doctor, a nurse, and a minister. Education was stressed by our parents for their children to turn out so successfully, and the next generation is continuing the tradition even better.

My husband earned degrees — bachelor's through doctorate — from four Michigan universities. Dad was in his glory sitting in Hill

Auditorium at the University of Michigan watching his son-in-law receive his doctorate. The experience was beyond his dreams.

Mom was a soft, gentle, kind Southern lady from Tennessee, reared in an area in which church was the center of the community, surrounded by farms of family and friends. Mom had five brothers and one sister, a very tightly knit group of family members who dearly loved each other and remained close throughout their lifetimes. When Mom was about nineteen, she was invited to Detroit to visit her brother, Lee, who had left the farm to seek work. It was at this time that Mom met Dad before returning to Tennessee, only to receive shortly thereafter a diamond engagement ring via U.S. mail. She accepted. The next time the young couple saw each other was on the occasion when Dad traveled to Tennessee to marry Mom. She was a hardworking mother at home, in the church, and at jobs outside our home. These jobs provided her daughters such things as spending money in college or a new dress for a party, or a new hat for Mom. The last job she had was at American Motors, in the private dining room of George Romney, who became governor of Michigan.

Mrs. Margaret Reilly and dad, 1943

When Dad died at ninety years of age, he and Mom had been married for sixty-five years. Mom also lived to ninety years.

My Uncle Lee, referred to above, reminds me of Dr. Ulrich; both were tall, handsome, kind, and gentle. Every time Uncle Lee and I parted, he said, "Sugar, if you need anything at all, just call me." Dr. Ulrich's parting words were, "Bless you." These men spent their lives helping people, friends and strangers alike — splendid examples of manhood, gentlemen.

My mirror reflects a precious family and friends: hardworking, honest, self-sufficient, unassuming. These loved ones honored family life, each other, and their friends faithfully throughout their lives. We always had time to help neighbors, those in need, and especially those who were ill. We were simple, God-loving people.

Mrs. Reilly's Uncle Al, Uncle Earl and father, 1920

Glaciers To Rivers

There are days
My hands are heavy
My legs are weary
My breath is shallow
As I lie down
I look forward to tomorrow
Knowing you are there
Knowing you care
I am grateful
For your love
For your friendship
May I always be
A memory
Of love
Of friendship.

Although it appears
So many years
Time is precious
For it disappears
I am grateful
For your love
For your friendship
May I always be
A memory
Of love
Of friendship.

Although it appears
So many years
Time is precious

Glaciers to rivers
Stones to sand
Father to daughter
Mother to son
Friend to friend
Although it appears
So many years
Time is precious
For it disappears
Love remains
Love remains.

There are days
My hands are heavy
My legs are weary
My breath is shallow
Although it appears
So many years
Time is precious
Glaciers to rivers
Stones to sand
I am grateful
For your love
For your love.

— Thomas P. Waldinger

Dr. Margaret Warrick

"I truly wanted to reach out to anyone in the audience who was dealing with something painful or sad and have their sense of spirit, if even for a moment, vicariously be in tandem with mine."

Of all of his patients, I, perhaps, have had the longest association with Dr. Waldinger. I began seeing Dr. Waldinger while he was a resident in training at the University of Michigan, and I was a graduate student, using the resources of the student health center. He treats my keloids (scar tissue that continues to form after trauma to the skin). The scars he has treated over the past eighteen years are somewhat a road map for the events that have shaped my life and reinforced my values and philosophies. These include unselfishness, empathy toward others, finding the positive in people and in difficult situations, and always maintaining a sense of humor. Though many people and experiences have reinforced and guided these values and philosophies, I primarily credit my father for teaching unselfishness and humility, my mother for imparting the value of always looking for the positive, a nurse for giving me hope, and my friends for reinforcing the joy and power of humor.

I grew up in the 1950s in a very secure and loving home. As the middle child, I had parents who never let me feel sorry for myself, even though I had an unsightly scar on my left arm. The early lesson in

finding good in bad involved this scar. My parents pointed out that I
was lucky because, with my scar, I could easily tell my left from my
right. When I was about eight years old, I was accompanying my dad
on his Saturday errands (something I always loved to do) when we
became lost and were suddenly driving through a very economically
depressed neighborhood. We came upon three kids trying to use an
old bike tire as a hula-hoop. My dad suddenly stopped the car and
opened the trunk where my sister's, my brother's and my hula-hoops
had been placed in preparation for a picnic later that day. He gave
those poor children the hula-hoops. I watched this action somewhat in
dismay. When my dad returned to the car, I looked at him with a combination of anger and pride. After all, he had just given away my hula-
hoop! I started to say something, but then he faced me, ready to
explain his actions. Suddenly I knew he didn't have to and then he also
knew he didn't have to. It was my first true lesson in unselfish giving.

While visiting my then-fiancé in San Diego in 1985, I was
involved in a near-fatal car accident. I won't go into all the details.
Suffice it to say, I gave Dr. Waldinger a whole new set of scars to work
on! Being on a respirator is probably the most horrible experience one
can have, next to thinking that death is imminent. Again, I touch on
the theme of unselfishness and the value of someone reaching out to
help another. About a day or two after I was taken off the respirator
and upgraded to intensive care, I became incredibly frightened about
death. It was late at night when Mary, an African-American nurse with
a beautiful round face, came into my room. I had never seen this nurse
before. She came to my bedside and asked if something was wrong and
why I wasn't asleep. I told her, with tears running down my cheeks,
that I was afraid that if I closed my eyes I'd never wake up again. She
took my hand and said that she would hold on to it, stay by my bed,
and make sure I didn't die. She was so sweet and so comforting, her
compassion and empathy so profound, that I trusted her and soon
drifted off to sleep. I never saw Mary again. I greatly wish that I could
because, more than the wonderful paramedics, surgeons, and physicians who treated me through this trauma, I credit Mary for giving me
hope and saving my life.

Surviving a traumatic car accident seems enough for one person, but in 1990, I heard those three dreaded words, "You have cancer." And, unfortunately, I heard those words two more times — in 1991 and 1994. Like one out of eight women, I have experienced breast cancer. My dealings with breast cancer have taught me persistence, humility, and the constant reminder that life is a precious gift and that

Dr. Margaret Warrick (left) with best friend Lynn, 1995

one should never take anything or anyone for granted. And, once again, I gave Dr. Waldinger new scars to work on.

It may seem odd to say this, but I think having had to deal with cancer has not been a curse, but a gift. I have this special secret. Unlike so many people who just go through life and sort of go through the motions, I know that one must truly live life. I was laughing with my best friend one weekend when visiting her in Cleveland. After a late Friday night with a very full day and evening ahead, I was up at 5:30 Saturday morning getting ready to make a six a.m. tee time with her husband. Lynn called out from their bedroom and said, "Marg, I can't believe you are doing this!" I poked my head in and, with a big smile, said, "Well, see, this is the curse of having had cancer. I feel compelled to live each day to the fullest!"

Besides teaching one to live life to the fullest, cancer also teaches you to keep the proper perspective on situations and challenges. I often think of a close friend who was diagnosed with breast cancer about a year before I was. Linda was not as lucky as I am. Many times when there is something I don't want to do or face, I think, "I bet Linda would rather be in my position than in her position." Unfortunately, Linda has passed away.

I also look to my mother, a recent widow, who has severe hearing loss and in the last year was diagnosed with macular degeneration. At eighty-three, she has incredible fortitude, energy, and spirit. She never feels sorry for herself; on the contrary, she continually remarks about how lucky she is to have great children and friends and her health.

Humor has played a major role in my life and I credit my parents, who both had great wits, and my plethora of friends who love to laugh. In even the most trying cases, one can find a humorous side, although this sometimes happens after the fact. Humor often is tragedy plus time. My closest friends never let me lose my sense of humor during my whole recuperative period after my car accident and during the three times I battled breast cancer.

Music and singing are also major forces in my life. I have always felt quite blessed that I could sing. Singing not only gives me a myriad of opportunities, but also provides me with a constant source of joy. It is hard to articulate the inner thrill I feel when performing great choral masterpieces such as Handel's "Messiah." When I was fairly certain that I was not going to die after my car accident, my fears turned to thoughts that I would never sing again. With a collapsed lung and most ribs broken, I had great difficulty breathing. I remember so clearly lying in that hospital bed, trying to come to grips with the thought that I would never sing the "Hallelujah Chorus" again. As the weeks and months slowly passed, the driving force for me in my recuperation became completing all the painful healing therapy not only to be able to stand up straight and walk, but also to be able to sing. After the June accident, I have never stood so proudly and with such humble gratitude to God as I did that following December when I stood on stage at Hill Auditorium in Ann Arbor and sang the "Hallelujah Chorus" with all my heart.

Of course, along with all my concern about singing, I worried about performing. In recent years I had become quite involved in Gilbert and Sullivan productions. To think that I would no longer be able to dance, move around on a stage, and experience the great joy of entertaining an audience were equally devastating. It was more than a year before I finally regained enough strength and mobility to be back on stage, performing in a lively Gilbert and Sullivan production.

I refused to let breast cancer interfere with performing, even though the director had to modify some of my movements. In the first production I appeared in after my first mastectomy, I was determined to succeed. Maybe because of pain, embarrassment, and fatigue, it is tempting to turn away from life, but because life is so precious, one has to turn into life, to embrace it. I remember returning to the stage after having recovered from my first mastectomy. I somehow wanted to be able to transmit to the audience a message that would have gone something like this: "Look at me. I am singing and dancing and making you laugh, and guess what? I've had cancer, and I'm beating it, and so can you! You can beat any obstacle, if you have hope and joy in your heart." I truly wanted to reach out to anyone in the audience who was dealing with something painful or sad and have their sense of spirit, if even for a moment, vicariously be in tandem with mine.

It was my encounters with cancer, and my realization that I was given a second chance the night that Mary held my hand, that prompted me to change my career course. These experiences gave me the necessary lenses to see clearly that one's life's work should be work that has human value. The measure of success in a career is not the size of a paycheck, but the opportunity to make a positive difference in people's lives. Recently, I left a prestigious but highly stressful position to take one in which I have the opportunity to impact children's lives. I'd like to think that I will have done my job well if I can impart to these children the critical values that have guided me in life and which I have touched on in the above biographical sketch. They are unselfish giving, finding the good in all situations and people, showing compassion and empathy toward others, keeping a positive outlook and attitude, and realizing the power of humor.

The Day You Were Born

Some day soon
When summer turns to fall
You will be weaving
A life of your own
So many changes
So many choices
Your smile still so sweet
When I hear you speak
I can feel
Love and joy
As the day you were born
As the day you were born.

There have been days
When you were the reason
To go on
In my solitude
I wrapped myself
In your love
With God
Anything is possible
As the day you were born
As the day you were born.

The struggles within
So many changes
So many choices
Will and endurance
Peace and kindness
Love and patience
Faith and gentleness

I wrapped myself
In your love
With God
Anything is possible
Anything is possible.

Some day soon
When summer turns to fall
You will be leaving
You will be weaving
A life of your own
In your solitude
In your struggles
When you feel yourself
Slipping away
Wrap yourself
In my love
With God
Anything is possible
Anything is possible
As the day you were born
As the day you were born.

Some day soon
You will be leaving
Your smile still so sweet
When I hear you speak
I can feel
My precious angel
In my arms
As the day you were born
As the day you were born
Anything is possible
Anything is possible.

— Thomas P. Waldinger

Mr. Cy Webber

"My parents set the example of love and consideration for each other that I have been able to use as a pattern to follow in my own life and marriage."

From the advantage of seventy-three years on this old earth, I have many rich memories that have brought beauty into my life. I was born in a very small town. At least it was a small town when I entered it — Preston, Idaho. Because of the Depression, we moved from Idaho to Kentucky. My youth was spent in those years called the Great Depression. Even though those years were hard ones, they were happy ones for me. While my dad never made a lot of money, he loved his family and we did a lot together. Family walks were one of our adventures. On other occasions, my mother would make a picnic and we would go to the park for an afternoon of fun and food. Once a month, if we could afford it, Dad would take the whole family to Moka's Restaurant. The owner, Harry, was a good friend of Dad's, and would always give us little goodies along with our meal.

My parents set the example of love and consideration for each other that I have been able to use as a pattern to follow in my own life and marriage. I was taught very early in life about the importance of God as a partner in life and of the many blessings we could receive if we followed His teachings. The teachings of Isaiah and of the Psalms became important to me. I remember that when I was in junior high school, a man used to come to the school once a month to our class and challenge us to memorize passages of Scripture. We would get a dime for every verse we memorized. The first I memorized was the Twenty-third Psalm because of its many verses (many to me as a youth). Therein began my love for the Scriptures and the book of Psalms.

Glenna and Cy Webber, newly engaged, August 1952

I met Glenna at Eastern Michigan University. We were married in our junior year and completed college together. We both entered the teaching profession and are now retired, having spent thirty years in a profession that has kept us young. We both taught at the high school level, dealing for the most part with wonderful teenagers. We have two sons and seven grandchildren, and all live close to us and we see them often. Both sons are successful in their employment and are a joy to have near us. On April 15, 1998, we celebrated our forty-sixth wedding anniversary.

Now, after forty-six years of marriage, I look back at the events in my life and realize the opportunities that have come to me have come because of the values and virtues I was taught and was willing to follow. We have learned the need to completely trust each other, to show love and affection for each other — even in front of our children, so they can see we are not ashamed of the love we share. We plan and do many things together. Though we have had many challenges in our married life, our trust in God and our ability to "roll with the punches" have given us the resilience to enjoy this beautiful world, even in adversity.

Dream With Me

You came into my life
A shooting star
In the midnight sky
A tulip opening
The first day of spring
A ray of sun
In the early morning
Upon my face
By God's grace
You came into my life.

River runs gently
To the sea
Sun rises slowly
In the east
With you in my life
A gentle peace
Life's mystery
Becomes harmony
Dream with me
Dream with me.

To be loved
And love in return
This I have learned
With you in my life
A gentle peace
A ray of sun
Upon my face
By God's grace
Life's mystery
Becomes harmony

Dream with me
Dream with me.

To be loved
And love in return
This I have learned
There is a place in my heart
For you always
You are a blessing in my life
A shooting star
In the midnight sky
A tulip opening
The first day of spring
A ray of sun
In the early morning
A blessing in my life.

Simplicity of thought
Serenity of being
Life's mystery
Becomes harmony
Dream with me
Dream with me.

— Thomas P. Waldinger

Mrs. Helen Long

"My approach to life is deeply rooted in my faith in God, acknowledging that God may not come when I call Him, but knowing that God will always show up on time!"

My parents were Harry and Gladys Hutchinson of Detroit, Michigan. I was the fifth of an eventual twelve children, having one older sister and three older brothers. We were poor, but we didn't realize it. It was the time of the Great Depression and we were in the same predicament as many of our neighbors. My father was an auto mechanic and my mother a homemaker. My mother "ruled the roost" and my father, a softie, was the peacemaker. To supplement our table, we grew and canned our own fruits and vegetables. Our home was always spotless and our clothes were always clean — this despite the fact that we did not have a washing machine and therefore used a washboard and hung our clothes on a line out of doors. I can remember my mother saying over and over again, "You only have one set of clothes; keep them clean!" and that we did. Even now, some seventy-one years and many sets of clothes later, I still adhere to her philosophy. Another defining character trait of mine that may be traced to the words of my mother is to "be friendly, but keep your distance."

In addition to family and home, there was a high priority placed on going to church and going to school. Church was and still is an important part of my life. Growing up, going to school was a given. I gladly went there to learn. Reading was my best subject. When I was young, I would often take a flashlight to bed and read while under the covers, late into the night. Today you will seldom find me without a book in hand. Sometimes I read two or three books simultaneously. As it was when I was a child, reading is my way of escaping to eras long past.

As the years went by, our family grew. Thank God, the economy also grew. As finances improved, so did our lives. We eventually moved into a home with a large yard, fruit trees, an enclosed back porch and enough room to comfortably house all of us. As I look back on this period of my life, I can remember coming home from church on a Sunday to find Daddy making ice cream, churning it on that back porch, and each of us kids jockeying to be allowed to lick the freshly made confection from the dasher. Even now when I close my eyes, I can still see this scene as clearly as if it were yesterday.

In 1945, I graduated from high school and began working as an employee of the city of Detroit. In 1950, I married John T. Long Jr., the love of my life. We were blessed with four children — one daughter, Michelle Yvette (1952) and three sons: John Thomas III (1955), Kevin Hutchinson (1959), and Michael Edward (1965). Michelle lives in Houston, Texas, with her attorney husband, Andrew McGhee. They are parents to two sons, Mari and Zachary. The Reverend John T. Long III lives in Daytona Beach, Florida, along with his wife, Maria, a corporate consultant, and their son, John IV. Their daughter, Nicole, is a sophomore at Wayne State University, Detroit. Kevin lives in Fort Worth, Texas, with his wife, Francesca, a student, and their three sons: Timar, a sophomore at the University of Texas-North, Kevin, and Jonathan. Michael and his wife, Courtney, still live in Detroit with their three daughters: Taja, Kyla, and Kyra.

In January 1985, my husband of thirty-five years suffered a fatal heart attack. I know that he is still watching over us and that he is as proud as I am of what each of our children has achieved. Our children are all married, all working, and all providing a good foundation for their own children.

John and Helen Long, wedding day, 1950

My mother-in-law, who passed away in August 1984, always used to say, "I may not have monetary wealth, but I am the richest woman in the world. I have the love of my grandchildren." I feel the same exact way. She taught me so much that has helped to sustain me. I have often said, "If I can be half the mother-in-law to my children's spouses that she was to me, they will have nothing to worry about." Daisy, you were the greatest!

In the 1980s, after suffering several years with a chronic and life-altering skin condition, I met the young Dr. Thomas Waldinger during one of my many stays at the University of Michigan Hospital, Ann Arbor. I found his bedside manner like that portrayed by doctors in the movies, only he was not acting out a role. He was a medical resident, studying to specialize in dermatology. We were doctor and patient and, over the succeeding years, we have become friends. My medical condition — prurigo nodularis — is indigenous to women of color or darker skin. I had given up all hope of wearing short pants and short-sleeved shirts ever again, but thanks to the unceasing efforts and medical care of Dr. Waldinger, my skin has cleared to the point that I can.

Once Dr. Waldinger submitted a paper to a dermatology journal concerning my condition and his conclusions. He is now in private practice and I see him on a scheduled basis. I am happy to say that under his care I have continued to improve. I am forever indebted to Dr. Waldinger for all that he has been able to accomplish in treating my condition. He is both a gentle man in temperament and a gentleman in character.

My approach to life is deeply rooted in my faith in God, acknowledging that God may not come when I call Him, but knowing that God will always show up on time! I know that without God I cannot do anything, and that my very life and the lives of those whom I love are forever in His hands. I rise every morning with a prayer of thanksgiving for my life. Regardless of the outside conditions, whether rain, sunshine or snow, I thank God every day for every day.

My daily prayer is that my children and their children will recognize the treatment of my condition as a blessing from God and that they will give Him all the praise and glory, for He and He alone is worthy to be praised. Amen.

In The Early Morning

In the early morning
Before the sun rises
Before birds sing
Before the moon sets
The meditation of my heart
The essence of my soul
Resides in your love
Resides in your grace
Divine peace.

In the early morning
When you are sleeping
I am praying
You will always be
In God's care
The meditation of my heart
The essence of my soul
Resides in your love
Resides in your grace.

In the early morning
I listen with my heart
I see with my soul
I hope you hear
Every moment of your life
I love you
The meditation of my heart
The essence of my soul
Resides in your love
Resides in your grace.

In the early morning
I find myself dreaming
We will rejoice
There is strength
In compassion
In love
In being gentle
The meditation of my heart
The essence of my soul
Resides in your love
Resides in your grace
Divine peace.

In the early morning
The sun is rising
Birds begin to sing
The moon rests until evening
My angel awakens
I hold you in my arms
You whisper
I love you
The meditation of my heart
The essence of my soul
Resides in your love
Resides in your grace
Clarity and peace
Love so sweet.

— Thomas P. Waldinger

Mrs. Elizabeth Leach

"What then would I tell my grandson and granddaughter if they were to say to me today, 'Grandma, tell us about your life'?"

I believe that there is a power greater than myself always available to me. I believe that within each of us is a God-given potential to be developed. My strength comes from my steadfast faith that I am never really alone and that the spirit of God within me will give me the strength and guidance to meet and to withstand whatever comes to me in life.

This all sounds like a very easy and simple philosophy. However, to actually live by this belief is not always easy. Fears, doubts, anger, insecurities, disappointments, illnesses, and losses of many kinds have confronted me and made it a challenge to stay on track to develop my potential to the fullest and to practice the faith I profess.

In my many years of life, there have been wonderful and happy times with many advantages and opportunities. There also have been disadvantages and lonely and depressing times. What then would I tell my grandson and granddaughter if they were to say to me today, "Grandma, tell us about your life"? The first things that would come to me would not be the sad parts of my life. Rather, I would probably tell them of how I grew up on a farm — loving, laughing, and "fighting" with my three brothers. I entertained myself walking rail fences, climbing in haymows, and playing barefoot in the river that ran through the back of our farm. Stories of how we would be snowed in for several days in the winter would also be included. This gave us a real opportunity for family togetherness. I still have fond memories of the taffy, fudge, and popcorn being made during these times and I remember the real happiness of looking up the road and seeing a snow-plow coming to free us.

Among these stories, it must not be forgotten that there were always chores around the farm to be done and each family member had definite responsibilities. Somehow, I would want my grandchildren to know how the activities at the little church in the village played an all-important part in the person I am today. One of the most significant stories would include my loving, hardworking, creative, and devoted parents who gave me support during good times, lonely and uncertain times, and also during the times I would want to try my wings and do new things.

This example stands out in my memory. I very much wanted to play in the high school band. However, we could not afford to buy an instrument. My mother came up with the idea that she would give me a hundred baby chicks to care for during the summer. In the fall, I sold the grown chickens and proudly bought a new clarinet. Playing in the high school band gave me a feeling of fulfillment and self-worth.

I may include in my stories the fact that my leg was in a cast and brace during the ages of three to seven. I still remember when, at the end of the four years, the doctor had me walk across the room. When he saw that my leg was straightened and healed, he said to me, "God has performed a miracle." That statement from the doctor has had an influence on how I've tried very hard always to develop my potential to the fullest.

I would hope that from these stories, lessons would be learned. These would include the lessons of the importance of being creative in the environment in which we find ourselves, by seeking out interesting things to do, and not always having to depend on others to entertain us. Also, it is important to know how happiness can come from doing simple things. I would stress the importance of belonging and of helping others, and the importance of knowing what is expected of us by having responsibilities and chores to do. Moreover, I would include the lesson of the significance of making commitments to oneself and to others and how all these things work together to give us a good self-image and a feeling of self-worth.

Mrs. Elizabeth Leach, 1997

Random Closing Thoughts

The clouds in your life can make beautiful sunsets.

Know yourself and be true to yourself.

Learn from your experiences — both good experiences and not so good ones.

Don't expect other people to please you all the time.

Don't feel that you always have to please other people all the time.

It is impossible to make everyone like you all the time.

Don't depend on other people for your complete happiness. We should not give others the burden of making us happy. Develop deep inner resources upon which you can always depend.

I try to remember that real happiness can come from knowing who we are. I believe that knowing myself and understanding what kind of a person I really am, and knowing what kind of a person I want to be are imperative in developing my potential to the fullest. To develop your potential is an ongoing process.

Try to learn something useful from all experiences.

Use blame and criticism from others as stepping stones to add still another dimension to your philosophy of life.

Keeping the right attitude is of utmost importance in living a happy and fulfilled life. Our attitude toward ourselves, toward others, and toward situations is very important. Actually, almost any problem in life can be made easier to face and solve by having a positive yet realistic attitude toward it.

In closing, I would like to say that people need the love and fellowship of other people. God works through us to make this world a better place.

Ocean Of Lilies

Imagine with compassion
Dream with love
Ocean of lilies
Sea of peonies
River of roses
Waterfall of daisies
The hand of the Almighty
Created diversity
Multitude of colors
For all to celebrate
For all to cherish
Dream with love
Imagine with compassion.

Mountains of wildflowers
Sun setting on the water
Waves of leaves
Snow dancing before its rests
Circle upon circle
Life upon life
The hand of the Almighty
Created diversity
Multitude of colors
For all to celebrate
For all to cherish
Live with courage
Dream with love
Imagine with compassion.

Life is a destination
Mystical and magical
Sorrow and struggle
A child is born
Grandmother is called home
Circle upon circle
Life upon life
The hand of the Almighty
Created diversity
Multitude of colors
For all to celebrate
For all to cherish
Live with courage
Dream with love
Imagine with compassion.

— Thomas P. Waldinger

Mrs. Betty Coogan

"A simple toy can bring you a lot of fun and love."

Since the death of my husband from lung cancer almost three years ago, I've had a lot of time to think and reflect on my life. There have been many lonely hours with nothing more to do than think and remember and get through the grieving.

I have been blessed with three sons and daughters-in-law, seven grandchildren, four sisters, two brothers, and many, many nieces and nephews. They have been very kind and helpful to me in many ways.

There is one favorite nephew who stands out among them, named Dave. He too has suffered greatly and has had a lot of sorrow in his young life. When he comes over to visit me, we find ourselves sitting in the kitchen having coffee and doing a lot of talking and soul-searching about the family, feelings, and memories. Somehow he has been a mentor to me. For a young man he has a lot of common sense and wisdom. He gave me the courage to go on with my life and do the things I want to do, and I love him for that.

One day I was talking to Dave about my childhood. I remember as a small girl looking forward to Christmas. It was during the

Mrs. Betty Coogan, on swing, 1939

Depression years and our family was on welfare like so many others. There were no gifts because we had no money. I'm sure my parents felt terrible but there was nothing they could do. At that time there were ten children — four brothers and six sisters. I was the youngest. My parents had emigrated from Italy in 1910. They both came from poor families so hard times were nothing new to them.

Christmas morning came and, to our surprise, the Goodfellows came to our house and brought each of us a gift. Mine was a beautiful, colorful rubber ball. I was so happy with that ball! It brought me much joy, love and happiness. I have never forgotten that Christmas.

I told Dave that is why I always purchased my children and grandchildren rubber balls to play with — large, small, and colorful ones. I would spend many hours playing games with them and enjoying their laughter. A simple toy can bring you a lot of fun and love.

When I was through talking, Dave said to me, "Aunt Betty, what a beautiful story you just told me about your life. Without even being aware, you were sharing and giving the gift of love to your children and grandchildren because that is what that rubber ball did for you on that Christmas morning." He was so right! I never saw it so clearly before. It was another one of the moments of our sharing our feelings that really helped me to grow and discover myself as the person I really am with a lot of love to give my family.

Now that I am older, I still love seeing children play ball. Whenever I go shopping and see colored balls in the stores, I can't help but smile. I remember how the gift of love, through a simple rubber ball, brought so much happiness to one little girl on that Christmas Day so long ago. That memory continues to extend the gift of love to me and my family today.

Rush Into My Arms

Rush into my arms
My bundle of joy
My bouquet of flowers
Precious angel of ours.

You couldn't wait
To enter this world
On that special day
Gentle spring showers
For my bouquet of flowers
Precious angel of ours.

Rush into my arms
Your first steps
You couldn't wait
To walk and play
To laugh and smile
To love and dream
And in between
A hug and kiss
You never miss
A chance
To share your joy
To share your love.

Rush into my arms
Our first dance
I imagine and dream
I am with you always
By your side
Cheering you on

Reach for the brightest star
Run the greatest distance
With love in your heart
Dancing always, never apart
Dancing always, never apart.

Rush into my arms
Our first dance
You never miss
A chance
To share your joy
To share your love
A gift from God
To see the world again
With love in your heart
Dancing always, never apart.

Rush into my arms
My bundle of joy
My bouquet of flowers
Precious angel of ours
A new beginning
Loving and living
A gift from God
To see the world again
With love in your heart
Dancing always, never apart.

— Thomas P. Waldinger

Mr. Roy Miller

"The insignificance of each member of society may seem obvious, but I subscribe to the oft-quoted Einstein phrase, 'Astronomically speaking, man is insignificant yet he is the astronomer.'"

I grew up in the depth of the Great Depression on the edge of the destitute Appalachian plateau. During my childhood I was keenly aware of the safety and support of the extended family, especially under adverse conditions. As Germany completed the capture of Europe and drove England back across the English Channel, I eagerly joined the Army Air Corps.

Life in the military acquainted me with the necessity for extensive cooperation between large groups of unrelated individuals who served a common cause. As one member of a ten-man crew on a B-17 bomber over the Reich, I painfully realized how precious life is. The only chance for survival depended primarily upon luck, aided in a small way by the skill and cooperation of my fellow crew members.

Suffice it to say, WWII ended favorably for me and the GI Bill extended opportunities beyond my wildest dreams. I gloried at my privilege of being alive and was profoundly awed at the mystery behind the scheme of things. It appeared to me that society was composed of groups of mankind acting much like individuals and unconsciously following a pattern like water running downhill.

I realized I wanted to devote my remaining life to raising a family while performing work in which I might possibly contribute to society in a basic manner. I decided I should train to teach physical sciences at the beginning college level where the young adults are searching for a foothold among their fellows.

Mr. Roy Miller, 1980

I met my future wife my first day in college and later, with her support and three children, accepted a teaching position at a junior college. Teaching has been a stable lifestyle and the remuneration sufficient to support a family with reasonable comfort. The children have all joined the professions upon completing college and have families of their own. My wife and I enjoy retirement immensely and the results of some forty years in the classroom have allowed a life more grand than I ever dreamed possible.

To spend a working lifetime as a teacher with young adults, continually dealing with man's discoveries and current concepts of the physical universe, has been completely satisfying. My duties have allowed me to conduct a class each semester for the non-science major. A majority of these students were preparing to be elementary teachers and thirsty for knowledge of how progress in mathematics, physics, chemistry, geology, and astronomy continues to open new avenues of approach to the mystery of our universe.

In studying this area of knowledge, a student invariably recognizes the contributions of great minds of the past and their relation to the societies in which they lived. It becomes apparent that individuals can progress in their search for meaning to their existence only through the support and resources of society as a whole. We live in a time when transportation, communication, and machines have aided mental processes and have abruptly changed the controls civilization has developed for all living relationships on earth.

I believe each person should be encouraged to contemplate the mystery of the universe and develop a desire to further a search for some comprehension. I am satisfied that my choice of teaching has allowed me to give some stimulus to those searching. An individual's contribution toward finding a place for man in the "Big Scheme" is a responsibility we all feel. As we shoulder the burden, society as a whole benefits. The insignificance of each member of society may seem obvious, but I subscribe to the oft-quoted Einstein phrase, "Astronomically speaking, man is insignificant yet he is the astronomer."

"The contemplation of celestial things
will make a man both speak and think
more sublimely and magnificently when
he descends to human affairs."

— Cicero

Dr. Robert L. Funaro

"In that silence, there is, at least for me, great wisdom."

There are times when I find myself asking key questions and reflecting on values, beliefs, and the mysteries of life. I just celebrated my sixtieth birthday, which set off in my mind a host of thoughts about six decades of learning to live with life and entering in the mystery of death. I put these two thoughts together because I have come to believe that in life there are many paradoxes and one of the paradoxes I see is that death and life have the same dynamics.

Breathing and not breathing, not-breathing leading to a new way to live . . . the fear of death is the fear of life, and the fear of life stops us from actively dying. I have learned to "listen to the whisperings" of life and the "whisperings of death." In my life, I often have stopped the race of life so that I can enjoy the silence that gives me peace, the silence that challenges me to draw deeper into the mystery of living. Some two years ago when a single "bump" on my head led me to hear that I might have cancer, I had a "whisperings" moment. All of the human fears emerged — what would I tell my wife, my children, my family? How would we cope? Where would my journey end and what were the processes that I was about to enter into? Then I practiced what I preached and stopped while I listened to the world around me. It said, "Bob, you are here . . . live today." The fear of not living was stopping me from living. I did not like that feeling or that thought.

I must say that Dr. Tom's gentle, peaceful way of helping me understand all the possibilities, combined with the thoughts of the other patients in his book, were "whispering" moments for me. I stopped, I listened, and I heard again about the value, the power, and the peacefulness of living the moment and preparing for the future. I was rejuvenated, revitalized and reenergized to relive the paradox. Would I die? Of course — it is a fact of life! There would be a time when God would challenge me to let go and transition to a fuller life. I believe again that seeing my Creator would "take my breath away" and draw me into an eternity of sharing, listening, loving, and being absorbed in the true processes of "living" life. If this was not the time, then I believe that I had been given the time, the opportunity to listen to more messages of life that would help me to prepare for my death and thus prepare for my "new day" of life. I have always believed that the more we open ourselves up to life's possibilities, the more ready we are to journey into the timelessness of death. That does not frighten me any longer. In fact, I have come to understand that what is most frightening is not living life fully. It is good for me to open myself to life's lessons and to hear that message. I believe that sometimes we need to just stop the race and pace of life and listen to the messages of the whisperings! In that silence, there is, at least for me, great wisdom.

> *"There is in all things an inexhaustible sweetness and purity,*
> *a silence that is a fountain of action and joy. It rises up in*
> *wordless gentleness and flows out to me from unseen roots*
> *of all created being."*
>
> — Thomas Merton

Mr. Joseph Koss

"We made paper footballs or taped up baseballs that were discarded by sandlot teams. These baseballs and footballs were used in 'real championship' games that far overshadowed today's World Series games or the Super Bowl."

It is difficult to place a value judgment on one's personal beliefs. The reason is that the influences of church, family and society combine with these values and blend them into a unique individual with unique personality characteristics. In fact, if I were to summarize these characteristics and draw from my lifetime experiences, I would have to say that a healthy individual would have to possess the virtues of good, prudential thinking that will discern right from wrong, as well as love and compassion toward others.

In judgment of my life's work, both as a supervisor at General Motors and later as an electrical instructor at Henry Ford Community College, I have found myself richly rewarded by working with people and helping them with some of their problems. In evaluating my personality and its development, I find that the love shown by my parents was a dominant factor. My parents immigrated to America in 1917 from the small state of Slovenia, Austria. Once settled in Detroit, they married and I am the youngest of their four sons.

I grew up during the Depression, which saw my father without work for seven years. Times were tough and survival seemed marginal

Mr. Joseph Koss at daughter Diane's wedding reception, 1988

at best. Fortunately, the combined unity and caregiving of families and neighbors made survival more of a certainty. The lack of monetary wealth seemed to manifest itself into family closeness and love. It created times of personal family humor as well as times of creative expression. I still recall having to make my own toys. An example of this was carving human shapes out of wood and making toy cars to park in cardboard boxes located beneath the furniture in the living room.

During the Depression, sports heroes were important to young minds. Trying to emulate these heroes led not only to creativity but also necessity. We made paper footballs or taped up baseballs that were discarded by sandlot teams. These baseballs and footballs were used in "real championship" games that far overshadowed today's World Series games or the Super Bowl.

Christmas was always a special time for us. The season started on December 6. That's when St. Nicholas would visit us and give a report to Mom and Dad on how good we had been during the year. If we were good, he would leave us a little gift, usually a bowl of fruit.

In later years, I carried on this tradition with my own family by having them put their shoes outside their bedroom doors on December 6. This custom was used well into our children's teen years. In fact, I surprised my oldest daughter when she was a junior in college. On December 6, I located her car in the dorm parking lot and put a large boot filled with fruits and candy in it. The following morning, the response was immediate. My daughter called her mother, asking where Dad was last night. To this day, she relates to her friends the time when St. Nicholas visited her when she was in college and how significant it is to always put your shoes outside the bedroom door on December 6.

In the final analysis, I have lived a full life, a truly meaningful life in which I can credit the hard times for giving me a sense of humor and a respect for humanity.

"In the final analysis, the question of why bad things happen to good people translates itself into some very different questions, no longer asking why something happened, but asking how we will respond and what we intend to do now that it has happened. . . . the ability to forgive and the ability to love are the weapons God has given us to enable us to live fully, bravely, and meaningfully in the less-than-perfect world."

—Harold S. Kushner

Mrs. Pat Barnes

"I figure that life has three very important elements:
time, energy, and memory."

"It ain't the life, it's the liver," said Mother Alphonsine, the Mistress of Novices. I was nineteen years old and had been in the convent for one year. After nine months as a postulant, I had received the beautiful blue habit of the Sisters, Servants of the Immaculate Heart of Mary — a blue habit and a white veil. In two years I would take the vows of poverty, chastity, and obedience and be allowed to wear the black veil of a professed sister.

The convent gets a lot of bad press. When I hear people talk about dried-up old nuns with a mean streak and a semi-automatic wooden ruler, I wish they could have had a peek inside Mother Alphonsine's novitiate.

She was a tall, big-boned woman in her fifties. Her posture was impeccable and her glasses as thick as Coke bottles, but she had a smile that lit up a room and a warmth that put even the most nervous novice at ease.

During recreation hour, she could be talked into a demonstration of Irish step dancing or — this was our favorite — she would read to us. There was one particular story, I think it was called "Mosquito

Ranch," that got her laughing so hard tears ran down her cheeks. She'd have to stop reading, pull off those thick glasses, and wipe her eyes. Sometimes we were all laughing so hard at her and at the story that she just plain couldn't continue.

Mother Alphonsine had a motto for every occasion. When I bumped into the Christmas tree and a lovely glass ornament crashed on the highly polished tiles, her immediate response was, "Sic transit gloria mundi" (Thus passes the glory of the world). If a novice seemed lonesome or down in the dumps, you could count on Mother Alphonsine to say, "A smile is cheaper than electricity, and it makes the home much brighter." She had volumes of these little snippets of wisdom on the tip of her tongue, but my very favorite was, "It ain't the life, it's the liver."

At first it stuck in my mind because the flawless grammar of our novice mistress had been invaded by the unspeakable "ain't." It was a good attention getter. As I pondered the meaning of the saying, I came to understand some of what she was teaching. Every person's life is packed with choices and challenges. You make your life what it is by what you choose to focus on. Like editors, we build up the scenes we select as important and minimize or forget what we don't want to be part of our life, our masterpiece.

I figure that life has three very important elements: time, energy, and memory. It's up to us to decide how we will spend our precious time and energy and what memories we will either dwell on or downplay. I think this is how we build our lives, and I am so grateful to Mother Alphonsine for the funny little saying that started me thinking in this direction.

I left the convent after ten years. It was a peaceful parting, no bitterness and no rancor. On the contrary, I am grateful for the excellent education I received, for the wonderful women I met, and especially for the time I was given to think.

Mother Alphonsine died about five years ago. I think she must have been well into her eighties. She had been responsible for the formation of hundreds of young novices, all of whom are now eligible for AARP. I wonder how many of them remember, "It ain't the life . . ."

"The Navajo teach their children that every morning when the sun comes up, it's a brand-new sun. It's born each morning, it lives for the duration of one day, and in the evening it passes on, never to return again. As soon as the children are old enough to understand, the adults take them out at dawn and they say, 'The sun has only one day. You must live this day in a good way, so that the sun won't have wasted precious time.' Acknowledging the preciousness of each day is a good way to live, a good way to reconnect with our basic joy."

— Pema Chödrön

Mrs. Marion Simmons

"I learned in childhood that everyone is respected, and we share what we have, however little it may be, with those who have less."

I lived and grew up in the 1930s in Philadelphia with my parents and sister. My parents had suffered losses in 1929 when the economy collapsed, as did many others.

In the early years of the 1930s, before I was in school, there were many peddlers coming to the house. They weren't beggars, as they had had homes and families and jobs, but were now homeless. They put together small sewing kits and kits of other small household items, so an exchange was made with a few pennies for a spool of thread or some pins. I remember the small pile of pennies that was kept on the table by the front door. No one was turned away empty-handed. Two or three pennies were given and a kind word. Sometimes on cold winter days, the peddler was invited in to get warm and have a small bowl of homemade soup. My mother listened well as they talked of their former lives.

When we were older and in school, our classmates were our friends and playmates. In winter, we went sledding, and when we were older we went ice skating on frozen ponds. In nice weather, we roller-skated; the skates were metal, clamped to one's shoes, and were tight-

Mrs. Marion Simmons, 1988

ened with a key. Double Dutch jumping rope and an infinite variety of other activities that children make up as they go along were enjoyed by us. The boys always seemed to play baseball. On rainy days, we played board games or cards in one or another's house. For us, growing up in the 1930s, it was the best of times. For adults, it was the Great Depression.

When we were older, we found that we could go anywhere in the city on our own and not be afraid. The city was very well kept and we liked it. It wasn't very crowded; traffic was slight because everyone used the bus, trolley, or elevated train/subway. As we expanded our horizons, we found that people were pleasant, considerate, and polite. It was automatic to do "little acts of kindness." That was the way the country was.

The United States is very generous. Whenever or wherever there's a need, there is the country with money, equipment, and people to help. It takes care of its own and has social and welfare programs to aid those who need it. The country and the government are made up of people. So they should act as we do.

I learned in childhood that everyone is respected, and we share what we have, however little it may be, with those who have less. We care about, and care for, our fellow man. It would seem then that living is generosity, and no one is left out or forgotten. There is no better way to live and not a better place in which to do it.

*"Humanitarianism is a link that binds together all Americans. . .
Whenever tragedy or disaster has struck in any corner of the world, the
American people has promptly and generously extended its hand of
mercy and help. Generosity has never impoverished the giver; it has
enriched the lives of those who have practiced it. . . . And the bread we
have cast upon the waters has been returned in blessings a hundredfold."*

— Dwight David Eisenhower

Mr. Weslie Williams

*"First child, bought first home and a car, and
went to work for the first time in a factory."*

As I look back on the decade of the 1940s, more things happened then than any other decade I can remember. In 1940,
my twin brother and I left Kentucky and headed for parts
unknown in Detroit. It was there I got my first job. In 1941, when
Japan attacked Pearl Harbor, war and the draft were uppermost in my
mind. Then, in 1942, I signed up for the draft and waited to be called.
I got my call in 1943 and was sent to Fort Leonard Wood, Missouri.

Furthermore, in April 1944, I was married and, just two weeks
later, was called to go to Camp Hampton Road in Virginia. There we
were shipped to Oran, Africa. We stayed there until we shipped out to
Italy. I traveled from the southern part of Italy to the north before the
war was over.

The year of 1945 brought the news that my daughter had been
born. It was good news because everything went well. Coming home,
seeing my wife, my daughter, and more of my family was really great
later that same year. That year was a "first" — first child, bought first
home and a car, and went to work for the first time in a factory.
Nothing much happened until 1948 when we had another child, a
boy. In 1949, I bought a brand new home and moved with the help of
friends.

76

Sometime after I had been home for a while, my wife, Ora, showed me a letter she had received from the chaplain of our outfit. He wrote that I was okay. What he had written in that letter reminded me of the time my buddies stopped on a road in an old truck and a chaplain stopped to ask how we were. I thought it was unusual that an officer was seemingly searching us out. We talked a bit and then he was on his way. I never knew until I got home that he had received a letter from my wife and was looking for me. He had answered her letter.

"The capacity to care is the thing that gives life its deepest significance."

— Pablo Casals

Mr. Weslie Williams, wartime photo, 1943

Anonymous Patient

"High on the list of wonders is that of being able to associate with people of all sorts."

My personal philosophy of life is still under construction and I am not sure that it is ready to be described in ink on paper. I can tell you a little about it but I am unable to state it in a simple few words. When it is ready to reveal, however, it will express my desire to help all with whom I have any association so that they will find only betterment of their lives from the association.

Just how this philosophical bent came to be mine I cannot say. Looking back, I can recall some terrible moments that should have made me quite bitter in life. As a five-year-old boy, I was abandoned by my mother. I can still remember the moment that she left our home. There was no one there except me at the time. It must have been as terrible a moment for her as it was for me. I remember that she promised to bring me an airplane when she returned.

My upbringing was left to my father and my grandmother. One winter and spring, the little country town of my school years fell victim to a siege of illness transmitted in the drinking water. Typhoid, diphtheria, and scarlet fever killed one-third of the children in the town. I was afflicted with diphtheria and scarlet fever but I survived.

I was left a not very well-developed child who took a long time to recover. I became "bookish," according to my friends.

The Great Depression of the 1930s tested our little family. I didn't realize it at the time, but it was teaching me how to survive on a very low economic scale. High school was an awakening for me and I enjoyed every one of its facets. One of the teachers took a special interest in my case and to my delight was instrumental in my obtaining a four-year scholarship at a prestigious university. It was a tough struggle but four years later I graduated with honors. I found a wonderful girl as a loving wife and we started a family. A career in electrical engineering and applied physics was well under way when World War II took over. My time in service was short but it was a soul-searing event. My wife preserved the family while I was away. I came home and wrapped myself up in their love. She was a lifesaver.

I have every reason to be less than generous in my attitude toward life. But strangely, it is just the opposite. My Creator has, I believe, tested me more than once. But He gave me recuperative powers that have carried me through some rough times. In addition, He gave me a wonderful and loving wife who has tolerated my lifestyle with grace.

My philosophy is very simple. To be alive and able to appreciate the wonders of Creation is a pleasure for me. High on the list of wonders is that of being able to associate with people of all sorts. I receive much personal pleasure in communicating with people. When first I meet someone, I enjoy evaluating the nature of the contact. At first the contact is a guarded one. It is as though one is viewing the new contact while being shielded behind a protective screen. Then as the nature and intent of the contact are made clear, the screen becomes less and less restrictive (or more so) as one's judgment commands. It is a kind of game. As the screen becomes less restrictive, the association becomes more productive. One must remember that each individual is a very complex product of our Creator's genius and it is a real privilege to have an unguarded exchange with each of them. There is something to be learned from every one of His creations.

"Life's greatest achievement is the continued remaking
of yourself so that at last you know how to live."

— Winfred Rhodes

Mrs. Jean Van Faasen

"The years have accumulated and so has the peace."

With the gift of seniority in years, we often find the answers to questions we asked in earlier life situations and can say, "Now I understand." My life did not follow a path I would have chosen. I would have selected a route devoid of troubles and ills with happy progress markers all along the way. Life is rarely so trouble free.

Major and minor detours occurred on my path, requiring great personal introspection and acceptance of situations I could not change. As I struggled against the changes, it was a turmoil I could not, or did not, share with others. My questioning was endless and without answers.

Realizing I was being forced to return to a career that I had happily abandoned to raise a family, I timidly approached combining a career and responsibilities of home. The challenges continued and increased, but amazingly so did my strengths. Along the way, I learned I could share my strengths with others as I often sensed the turmoil they masked behind their response of "I'm fine, thank you." Life prod-

ded me and molded me to try harder, look deeper, be more understanding, and recognize the often difficult paths others are traveling.

Now I understand what life was trying to teach me and I am grateful for the passage, though rough at times. The years have accumulated and so has the peace. It is a lovely gift.

"To be what we are, and to become what we are capable
of becoming, is the only end of life."

—Baruch Spinoza

Mrs. Jean Van Faasen, 1996

Mr. Carley Tolliver

"I believe our lives should be lives of service — that we owe to our Creator a responsibility to all mankind as well as to the earth upon which we live."

I was born December 11, 1931, in Whitaker, Kentucky. It is a small town between Hazard and Pikeville. The post office was South East Coal Company. I was the second of nine children. I grew up in a rural farming area raising hogs and chickens, and growing most of our own food. I learned how to raise and care for animals and to grow a variety of crops.

My father had an ice business, and part of my responsibilities was helping him with ice delivery to both homes and businesses. I had all the childhood diseases in my early school years and missed a lot of school due to sickness. I was always the smallest and skinniest kid in my school class. I weighed only ninety-eight pounds in high school.

I believe our lives should be lives of service — that we owe to our Creator a responsibility to all mankind as well as to the earth upon which we live. Each person should leave this earth a better place than he or she found it. A life should have a positive rather than a negative effect. If the peoples of this world were true brothers and sisters as God intended, we could eliminate many of the problems in the world today. This type of interaction would benefit not only people, but

Mr. Carley Tolliver, avid photographer, surveys father-in-law's
peach trees, 1983

plants and animals as well. Very few of us see all the beauty in God's
creation.

I remember when I was very young (during the ending of the
Great Depression), I became aware of my responsibility to
others. My father brought a young man home for dinner. This man
had left his home looking for work because his parents and his family
were desperately in need. My mother cooked an excellent dinner and,
as we ate, with tears he told his story and expressed how wonderful it
was to find people as kind as my parents. She always had a gift of listening and being able to cheer the hearts of those in need. As I listened, I became more and more conscious of the needs of others and
developed great pride in my parents. I realize that I have patterned my
life always to be aware of the needs of others. My parents (mostly my
father) later helped the young man find a job.

Our family was very religious and I followed their example. Sunday morning at our house, as with many rural mountain people of eastern Kentucky, found us preparing for a day of church-going and religious devotion. We always had guests for Sunday dinner, and I enjoyed listening to their conversations and learning more about people.

Moreover, my mother possessed a sense of cheerfulness and humor, which I also developed as I matured. She was always helping in the community to get help for the needy. Also, there was always company at our house and my mother listened and helped by collecting clothing for the needy, caring for the ill, and preparing and taking food to neighbors who were unable to prepare their own food. Many people called on my mother to pray for them and to sit with the bedridden. She could get more done in the community than anyone I ever knew.

In my junior high school years, I attended Hindman Settlement School in Knott County, Kentucky. This school was famous for what I already believed in — a life of service. Several nights during the week, great speakers would come to the Great Dining Hall and, after the evening meal, would give a short talk, or sometimes a long speech. We had good speakers who helped to mold my life and make my beliefs more steadfast.

During this time, I became acquainted with a great man, in my estimation — the Reverend J. S. Bell. I considered him to be totally dedicated to his work. He never retired, but continued his ministry until his death a few years ago. His taped messages are still played on radio stations in that area. Also, the founder of the Settlement School, Elizabeth Watts, further influenced my life. She always let me know that I was on the right track, so to speak.

I attended Caney Junior College at Pappa Passes, Kentucky. This was a small, nondenominational college in Knott County. Its founder, Alice Lloyd, was another great influence on my life. She was, furthermore, totally dedicated to the service of others. The college stressed what they called "The Purpose Road" — a life of service. Mrs. Lloyd sponsored many students who went on to the University of Kentucky at Lexington. She is responsible for many doctors, lawyers, teachers, ministers, and so on. She never retired, but worked all these years as an invalid, until her death. Mrs. Lloyd is listed in the "Who's Who" of dedicated women. She was on the Ralph Edwards television show "This is Your Life." Even today, Dr. Ralph Edwards serves as Trustee Emeritus on the Board of Trustees of the college.

With all these influences in my life, how could I believe or develop any differently than I have? All in all, it's the daily little things one does that really count. I met my wife, Josephine, at Caney College and she has a similar philosophy in life, so we have a lot in common. Our life together has been wonderful. We both feel that we have been positive factors in the world.

"The sole meaning of life is to serve humanity."

— Leo Tolstoy

Mr. Jack Stead

*"People I didn't know, and whose language I was unable to speak,
gave me food, clothes, shelter, transportation, and
a route over the mountains to Spain."*

I was shot down during the war and here is my offering. The plane takes off. It is 7:40 a.m., 13th Mission, Rattlesden, England, April 27, 1944. I was still a boy, married with a new daughter, but still a boy. Now I have grown up quickly. Life used to seem long, but now each day seemed as though it was going to be short.

This was to be an easy mission, back to base in four hours. Just over to France, drop bombs and return home.

We are hit with flak, on fire and falling. Bombs still aboard, we bail out. I hide and escape capture.

People I didn't know, and whose language I was unable to speak, gave me food, clothes, shelter, transportation, and a route over the mountains to Spain. I am free, alive, and can go home. Of all those who helped me, I only remember two.

From that day on, I considered each day a special gift and each person someone to help if they needed it. I never could repay those I really owed. I have had a wonderful life and enjoyed everything I have been able to do for other people.

The following is from a newspaper report in 1944:

SAFE

Staff Sergeant Jack W. Stead, 23, Fortress gunner, escaped via underground by walking several hundred miles after being shot down over France, April 27, 1944.

> *"Try not to become a man of success, but rather*
> *try to become a man of value."*

— Albert Einstein

Mr. Jack Stead, Air Corps Staff Sergeant, home on leave, 1944

Mr. Dale Anderson

"Even for the highest posts it is only in some cases application that is wanting, rarely the talent."

I think that it is fundamentally true that much important wisdom is acquired prior to school age. Unquestionably, the most significant values in my own life certainly were acquired at a very early age. In trying to remember life's earliest influences, I recall two little stories that my mother, at my insistence, would read to me over and over.

The first story was *The Little Red Hen*. This is a story of talking farm animals who taught others the wisdom that we must take responsibility for our own actions. The second meaningful story was entitled *The Little Engine that Could*. A small train engine in this book teaches that when we face up to our responsibilities by thinking positively, anything is possible. "I think I can, I think I can . . ."

Although it probably was not recognized among the earliest lessons learned, I have come to realize that the most important possession that anyone has is his or her character or name. It takes a long, long time to build a good character, but only seconds to destroy it. Good character will carry you to a satisfying life and is something that no one can take away without your cooperation. Character is built, bit by bit, in your day to day dealings with other people and with yourself. It

Mr. Dale Anderson, weekly seventy-five-mile ride in desert, Arizona, 1998

depends upon being honest and fair with others and with yourself. It requires that you respect other people, even if you do not like them. And it requires that you put forth your full effort and talents when given a job to do, whether or not someone is watching over you and whether or not you will receive a reward for completing the job.

Here are some helpful sayings and guidelines that, when conscientiously applied, will help us to acquire good character:

- Tell the truth
- Cleanliness is next to godliness
- Finish what you start
- Anything worth doing is worth doing well
- Give the benefit of the doubt
- Don't litter your mind or your environment
- All work and no play make Jack a dull boy
- Live according to the Ten Commandments and the Golden Rule

• Stabilize your life with a spiritual anchor
• Practice self-discipline.

A final piece of character-building wisdom was passed on to me in college by a mathematics professor who daily posted inspirational writings or quotes on the board. It is titled "Application and Ability." This writing emphasizes that there is no attaining eminence without both, and where they unite, there is the greatest eminence. Mediocrity obtains more with application than superiority without. Work is the price that is paid for reputation. What costs little has little worth. Even for the highest posts, it is only in some cases application that is wanting, rarely the talent.

"What do we owe a child?
Sustenance and shelter . . . roof and raiment.
What else?
A chance!
The best chance we can give to begin and to become.
A chance to get past rock and reef into the channel and
direction and control to survive the current.

What children need is a set of carefully crafted,
somewhat magical touchstones
which, in youth, transform into moorings,
giving first the security of place
and then giving growing vessels
a chance to be built strong in still water.

Later the touchstones transform again —
into paddle, rudder, and stern,
allowing fresh, new pilots to negotiate and navigate
the incredible currents of adult life.

The magic touchstones that children need,
and that parents owe,
are values —
values that hold us, secure us, guide us."

— Linda and Richard Eyre

Mr. Russ Gibb

"The coming together and sharing in a classroom discussion is a repast that lasts a lifetime."

It doesn't take long for a teacher to learn that if you listen carefully to your students, you will soon be carefully taught. After thirty-five years as a high school teacher, I have learned several important life lessons from my students.

First, never turn your back on your students. Think about it. The obvious meaning is the blackboard scene, with chalk and spitballs flying. Yet the deeper meaning is that students are young and developing personalities and have to know that someone will always listen and understand the trials and tribulations they are going through at the moment. Being a good listener is important both to the teacher and those he would teach.

The second is never miss a meal. Mealtime is important, but the most important meal is the fulfillment of intellectual feeding and the communal activity of breaking bread. Intellectual discussions with one's younger charges are as satisfying and fulfilling as Mom's Sunday dinner. The coming together and sharing in a classroom discussion is a repast that lasts a lifetime.

Mr. Russ Gibb, "Night Call," The Mutual Broadcasting Company
telephone radio talk show, Detroit, Michigan, 1972

The third is when students get excited about learning, get out of
their way. Over the years I have seen it happen. One student gets an
idea, and before long, others are talking about it. It spreads like a
prairie fire. The desire to learn and intellectual curiosity grow, and at
this point the teacher should be passive and let the students' curiosity
and zest for learning take them where it may.

Yes, over the years I have learned many things from my students.
They have taught me that immortality is not something carved in
stone or on plaques placed upon walls, but that true immortality is

when your shared ideas are engraved in the hearts and minds of your students.

The greatest lesson one can ever learn is to love and be loved in return.

*"The one exclusive sign of a thorough knowledge is
the power of teaching."*

— Aristotle

Mrs. Eleanore Smith

"I have discovered, during my eighty-five years of life, that anyone can accomplish what he wants if the will and desire are there."

I have discovered, during my eighty-five years of life, that anyone can accomplish what he wants if the will and desire are there. As a young woman, I was very sheltered and thought that life was only music and my cello. However, at thirty years of age, I lost my husband in the war and was left with a small baby boy. It was at this time that I found it was very important for me to bring up my child and instill in him the things that were most important to me. This meant no lying, being honest, no sneaking, no cheating and, above all, having good morals.

Of course, I wanted the best I could give him — not necessarily material things, but love and good values. Over the years I have found that there is always some good in everyone, if you stop to look for it. You do not always have to give material things, but only give of yourself.

Trust your own instincts and don't let others try to influence you. I worked hard at anything I could do to maintain a good life for us. It was not always easy, and I'm sure I have made many mistakes. But I have a wonderful son of whom I am very proud. Life is a great learn-

ing process. There may be a
lot of bumps along the way,
but friends and perseverance
are priceless. Don't ever give
up. Take what life offers you.
Take it graciously and don't
complain about the difficulties. Everyone has them!

Good friends are a won-
derful gift, but you also
must give of yourself and
you will receive. I'm back
again with my music and
cello and I certainly enjoy
sitting on the top of the lad-
der.

Mrs. Eleanore Smith and son Erik, 1948

Happy is the one who finds wisdom,
the one who gains understanding;

For its fruits are better than silver,
its yield than fine gold.

It is more precious than rubies;
no treasure can match it.

— Proverbs 8

Mrs. Mary Lou Gorham

"In her quiet way, she truly is an angel
walking here on earth amongst us."

Outside, it's a beautiful Michigan summer day. Inside me, it is stormy and mixed with so many different emotions and feelings. When I was asked to share my thoughts with others, I chuckled and said, "Why me — especially at this time of turmoil?"

Our older brother lost his wife to pancreatic cancer four weeks ago. This week, news came that our other brother has colon cancer. We are on our way now to Missouri as a family, to be with him and his wife for his surgery. Mom is scheduled for a repeat of surgery she had last summer. But instead of being another job I wasn't sure I had the time or energy for, writing this gave me the opportunity to put things back in place, restore my faith, and continue on. I thank you, Dr. Waldinger, for this. A calm has returned within me.

I have a loving, understanding husband and friend of forty-five years. Daily, Robert goes beyond the call of duty for his family and friends. We have two outstanding daughters and one son. Also, we have three lovely grandchildren, young in years and trying to find their way in life. So many wonderful blessings to be thankful for.

Our mother, Mrs. Okla Wales, is known as the "Angel Lady" at the senior apartment building where she lives. She makes and gives away angels by the hundreds. These are made and given with love to those she knows or just meets at a particular time or place in a person's life. Everyone who has met her, or has had the opportunity to know her, even briefly, will never forget her. She will be in their hearts forever. In her quiet way, she truly is an angel walking here on earth amongst us. We love her.

"May we be worthy to serve you."

— Blessed Teresa of Calcutta (Mother Teresa)

Dr. Robert Young

"Look back only to learn."

In the spring of 1998 at an appointment with Dr. Waldinger, he asked me about the things that have made a difference in my life. As I reflected on this question, there were three things that entered my mind. Three times in my life I had felt a compelling drive to put some thoughts on paper. At that point in life, two had been accomplished and one had not.

The first was a letter that I presented to my granddaughter on her twelfth birthday. After having spent a lifetime working with young people, I felt that I recognized some areas in her life which needed shoring up. The second time was a poem that I wrote to be read at my memorial service.

The third deals with a theory I developed early in my school administrative career: "The Relationship Between Perceived Love and Perceived Expectations in Adolescents." This theory guided me in my dealings with high school and junior high school youth as I worked with them, endeavoring to get them to apply themselves to the fullest extent possible.

Dr. Robert Young, school administrator

In October 1967, at the age of thirty-nine and with nine and a half years' teaching experience, I was appointed to the position of assistant principal at an urban high school. Prior to that I had grown up in a very loving home, survived two years in the U. S. Navy, spent two years working in a factory, and attended college. As I look back on this now at the age of seventy, I see that even though I was middle-aged in 1967, I had lived a rather sheltered life.

The position of assistant principal presented daily challenges so severe that for the first six months I left work every day with a severe headache. In addition to the headaches, I was learning much about the wide range of relationships that exist between adults (parents and teachers) and high school age youth.

One of the first insights I developed was that young people are very resilient to change, but one thing that the vast majority could not handle was the breakup of the family. Parents could move the family from house to house, from city to city, and from state to state, but tear apart the family and you have torn apart the only world the child knows and cares about. Over the years, I developed great respect for the couples who could put aside their personal differences and bite their lip until the children in the family were old enough to have left home before a breakup occurred in the family. Selfishness on the part of too many adults has left youth with nothing to hold on to and nothing to care about. Far too many young adults take too lightly the responsibility given them by the Supreme Being when they bring babies into this world.

And now the compelling theory which guided me in my many years as a school administrator. This theory was probably developed during the first three or four years I worked as a high school assistant principal. It was during this period that I first began to recognize the vast differences that existed in the relationships between parents and their children or teachers and their students. Before I go further, I want to state that this theory holds true for any adult who has a relationship with a young person, whether as a parent, grandparent, teacher, minister, or leader of a youth group.

Young people, even babies, have an innate ability to make judgments about their relationships with adults. They may not have accumulated in their brain the history of the human race, but they do have the ability to make a judgment regarding how little or how greatly an adult cares for them as a human being. The amount of caring that is displayed by the adult does not translate one-on-one to the caring perceived by the youth, and it is the amount of caring perceived by the youth that is key. The adult in this relationship must be able to relatively gauge this perception.

The second factor in this theory is the adult's expectations, which he or she can reasonably expect the young person to make a concerted effort to achieve. The greater the perceived love and concern flowing from the adult to the young person, the greater can be the expectations placed on the young person. It is the responsibility of the adult to perceive and keep in balance in the mind of the young person the relationship between the perceived love and concern and the perceived expectations of the adult. If the perceived love and concern are great, then the expectations can be great, but if the perceived love and concern are low, then the expectations should also be low. Get these two factors out of balance in the mind of the young person and problems arise.

To illustrate the above point, consider for a moment a young person who perceives great love and concern flowing from the adult to the youth, but the perceived expectations are very low. All too frequently this situation produces a young person we call "spoiled" — spoiled because the only expectation placed on the young person is to do his or her own thing and ask for what is wanted. Good grades or chores around the house are not expected. The attitude developed in the mind of the young person is that "I am so good that I can do whatever I please and get away with it."

Consider also the young person who perceives very little love and concern flowing from the adult, but yet the perceived expectations placed on the young person are very great. The relation on the part of the young person is rebellion: "Why should I do all this work for you? You do not care anything about me." Child abuse frequently comes from homes where the parents want their children to be good and do the right thing, but the parents do not have the ability to convey a message of love and concern for the child.

Through my twenty-five years as a school administrator, my years as a parent and grandparent, and as an observant adult, I believe that an adult who can accurately read these perceived relationships in the mind of a young person can significantly and predictably guide the maturation and development of the young person.

To Jackie on Time at Twelve

by Dr. Robert Young

On a cold, snowy day in December of 1980, you slipped out of your mother's womb and into this thing man calls time.

You brought with you no material possessions — no hat, no shoes, no blanket, no stocks or bonds.

Greater, however, than all the world's material possessions, you came in a body, with no parts needing to be recalled — a body in which you could travel through what man calls time.

Twelve years have passed since that snowy day, and you are now at the age where your journey through time will be guided more and more by you and less and less by Mom and Dad.

Some of your friends will think this means more freedom and, eventually, to be free at last, but always remember that you are never really free because you will always be responsible for the decisions you are free to make.

To make good decisions is often a difficult process, especially during the teens when the development of one's body outpaces the development of one's mind.

This body clock and mind clock inside each of us get out of sync for a short period early in our lives, but each of us must do our best to make good decisions in spite of this challenge.

Life, this passage through time, can often be tough and challenging but yet a beautiful and rewarding experience, or it can often be tough and challenging and a very depressing experience.

The decisions you make along the way will determine the kind of experience you will have in this thing called time, so strive to make good decisions.

You will not always make the "right" decision, but remember two things: You should always learn from your mistakes, and making a mistake would never change the love we have for you.

Growing up may be the most difficult thing you ever have to do, and the biggest mistake you can make is to be in a hurry.

When you are sixteen, make decisions of a sixteen-year-old and not the decisions of a twenty-year-old as so many young people do.

Getting a good education through college is the minimum foundation you will need for the challenges to be faced in your journey through time.

Know always that you have been loved from the moment you arrived, but know also that love does not dictate that those who love each other must always agree.

Finally, you need to know that this thing called time is nothing more than the movement of matter through space, the movement of the earth around the sun.

You need also to know that this movement has been going on for eons, and many before you have made the journey on which you have embarked.

At the end of this journey, we all depart with no material possessions, and we leave behind the body which inserted us into time, a body recalled only once.

Remember always that your mom, your dad, your brother, and your grandparents love you and want only the very best for you in your journey through this thing man calls time.

— Your Bubba

Opal and Robert Young with grandchildren,
Ryan and Jacklyn, 1989

Final Words

Mourn not for me that life is done;
My final adventure has just begun.
Reflect now on the life we've had;
It brought us both the good and bad.

Remember not the harder days,
But rather share our common ways.
Seek out today my living kin, and
Let them know just where we've been.

Speak out about the fun we had, and
Let them know that death's not sad.

Three goals were set to live each day;
I selfishly wanted my final pay.
To live my life as God saw fit,
I sought to give that extra bit.

To make the world a better place,
Has brought a smile to the human face.
To hear the laughter in your voice,
Was for me a daily choice.

To make you laugh has been one call;
It's your turn now to field the ball.

Thanks much, and look forward.
Look back only to learn.

— Dr. Robert Young

Dr. James Rynearson

"One of 'His Boys'"

I would like to share with you an incident of many years ago when two professionally trained men willingly shared their insight and encouragement with a most personable and academically talented young collegiate male.

The year was 1941 and in Ypsilanti, the then Michigan State Normal College had been preparing embryonic teachers for almost a century. One such student was a senior by the name of Victor Apple, who was majoring in physical education. This student's advisor was my father, Professor Elton J. Rynearson, who also served as athletic director and football coach and taught anatomy and physiology.

Elton Rynearson enjoyed his association with these young men and particularly those who participated on the college athletic teams. He followed closely "His Boys" as they went out into the world to provide their contributions. No doubt such a reward surely would have awaited Victor Apple had it not been for an unfortunate (or perhaps fortunate) injury to his knee during his senior year of collegiate football.

Immediately, Professor Rynearson contacted Dr. Carl Badgely of the Orthopedic Department at the University of Michigan Hospital.

He had always been so considerate of the Ypsilanti
college's needs, and he once
again rendered his service.
The diagnosis revealed an
avulsion of the knee known
as Osgood-Schlatter disease.
The necessary surgery was
performed and the injury was
basically corrected.

However, the story does
not end there. So impressed
was he by Dr. Badgely's skills,
duties, and good will, Victor
Apple qualified for and graduated from the University of
Michigan Medical School
and served as Dr. Badgely's
Chief Assistant. In his office

Dr. James Rynearson, 1973

on the ground level of the old University Hospital, Dr. Badgely placed
a picture of Victor Apple on the wall reserved for "His Boys."

"The divine guidance often comes when the horizon is the blackest."

— Mohandas Karamchand (Mahatma) Gandhi

Mr. & Mrs. Cornel Peleo

"Fifty years and two lovely daughters later, no sad songs for us."

Sweet Bird of Youth. The Golden Years are fleeing and memories never do.

As my husband and I reach our later years, we fondly recall the people and events that enriched our lives in the bar and restaurant business and the endless stories and Damon Runyon characters that made up our lives. We recall with amusement and sadness all of our departed friends who played a role in our lives.

My sister marvels at how my husband can spin countless stories of "cabbages and kings." Our parents, born in the "old country," also added to the folklore by telling of their adventures there. Needless to say, there were a few ghosts thrown in. There are endless marathons of old movie viewing along with listening to big band albums to reminisce, and as long as we can bring a little joy to the people we come in contact with, life is good!

Fifty years and two lovely daughters later, no sad songs for us.

Cornel and Florence Peleo in front of her father's barber shop,
Mike's Barber Shop, 245 Joseph Campau, Detroit, 1948

"Sooner or later we must realize there is no station, no one place to arrive at once and for all. The true joy of life is the trip. The station is only a dream. It constantly outdistances us.

"'Relish the moment' is a good motto, especially when coupled with Psalm 118:24: 'This is the day which the Lord hath made; we will rejoice and be glad in it.' It isn't the burdens of today that drive men mad. It is the regrets over yesterday and the fear of tomorrow. Regret and fear are twin thieves who rob us of today.

"So, stop pacing the aisles and counting the miles. Instead, climb more mountains, eat more ice cream, go barefoot more often, swim more rivers, watch more sunsets, laugh more, cry less. Life must be lived as we go along. The station will come soon enough."

— Robert J. Hastings

Mr. Arthur Shaw

*"We finished the hole and as we walked off the green,
I broke the silence with, 'Don, you had a problem.'"*

I learned my philosophy of life from a very dear friend named
Don Merryman. This man influenced my life in so many ways and
the effect that he had on me was truly profound. His attitude
toward life was wonderful. He was interested in people and his philosophy made me change the way I experienced life and how I was able
to cope with all the challenges that I had to face.

Playing golf with Don Merryman was always an enjoyable experience. He carried a twelve handicap at three country clubs: Washtenaw,
Dearborn and Whispering Pines, North Carolina. Playing golf with
him on a sunny day at Washtenaw was an event that I wish to share
with you. On the fifteenth hole, par four, Don had a fine drive
through the woods straight down the center of the fairway. However,
his second shot was short of the green and the ball went into the water
fronting the green. Don quietly opened a sleeve of new Titleist balls
and promptly hit the next three into the water. He then followed with
the second and third sleeves of three. He also proceeded to take the
fourth sleeve out of his bag without a word and went on to hit three
beautiful shots near the hole. We finished the hole and, as we walked

off the green, I broke the silence with, "Don, you had a problem." He answered, "Yes, but I solved my problem."

Don was a gentleman in every way. In our thirty years of friendship, he never used off-color words and never spoke of anyone except in a positive way. He also never told a joke that could not be heard by everyone. I wonder what he would think about our TV programs, our newspapers, and our world leaders and their actions today. Don's expression of anger was, "Dad bum it!"

He and his family visited all of our states. He wanted his children to know and see all of the country he loved. My wife, Maxine, and I built a home in Whispering Pines, North Carolina, next to Hazel and Don's with the desire to enjoy their friendship for many years. The loss of Don changed everything. We sold our home of ten years, never having lived in it.

About four years after we lost Don, a friend of his called me and said, "Art, I must tell you how I felt about your friend. If a man can

Maxine and Arthur Shaw, 1975

love a man, I loved Don." I loved Don also. This special man was close to his church and his contact with all people was one of caring. His years of work and service as a Rotarian tell much of him.

"It is well to think well; it is divine to act well."

— Horace Mann

Mrs. Arthur Shaw (left), golfing with the Merrymans, 1970

Anonymous Patient

"Pass it on. . ."

After much thought, I have decided there are several instances that helped form my philosophy of life. I am a Depression baby and was born in 1933. We lived in a suburb of Detroit and, as for most people during the Depression, money was short. Thank goodness, my dad was fortunate. He had a job that was necessary. This position was shared with two other people. The company they worked for allowed them each to work one day a week. Instead of two having no income, each had one day's pay. This helped with the necessities, but there was nothing left over for extras. I had an aunt who had no children, but had a steady job and was very generous. She provided us with many things whenever she could. The Depression ended, we grew up, and help from our aunt was no longer necessary. However, she was always around and always willing to help.

When my husband and I were married, he had just completed college, but I had not yet finished. He was from another state and I had not yet met his family. Money was very scarce. My aunt, however, was aware that we would like to make the trip to see his family. We were not sure that we could afford to travel, even by car. My generous aunt provided the means for the trip as a wedding present. My husband and I were very grateful, but did not know how we could ever repay her for her help throughout our life. She looked surprised and said, "Well, you were never expected to repay me. You are, however, expected to 'pass it on' if it is needed and if you are able."

My husband and I took this advice seriously. Throughout our life together, we have had several relatives who needed assistance and whenever we were able, we did "pass it on." I realized one day, to my delight, that not only had we helped when possible, but also we must have passed on the philosophy to the next generation. Shortly after our daughter married, there was a family gathering for our son-in-law's family. Apparently one of his younger relatives needed some help, and he and our daughter were providing some assistance. His father was cautioning him that they probably would not be repaid. Our son-in-law answered, "Oh, we do not expect to be repaid. My wife's family has a tradition that if one can afford to help, one does and, if repayment is not possible, then those helped should pass it on when they can."

My aunt died several years ago. We are very grateful that her philosophy has lived on and helped many others. Hopefully, the next generation will continue the philosophy started by my aunt years ago. It has been a lesson well learned.

"The best portion of a good man's life,
His little, nameless, unremembered acts
Of kindness and of love."

— William Wordsworth

Mr. Keith Harkins

"So I'll be a kid at heart and live each day as if it is my last."

What is my philosophy of life? I'm not really sure. The first thing that comes to mind is when I was a little boy and my mom let me paint my bedroom furniture. On the back of the chest of drawers I wrote, "Never give up, no matter what." This has helped me get through many hard times. I truly never give up, no matter what.

At the age of thirty, I lost my best friend of twenty years. I thought my heart would break. Knowing that there was something that I must learn from this, I knew that I must move on and not live in the past. Today, because of Greg's death, I look at each and every day as a gift from God.

Although I'm not sure that there is a proper way to pray, I like to get down on my knees and thank God for every day He has given me. I have learned to take full responsibility for my mistakes, deal with them, and focus on today. The truth is that we can only count on today. Yesterday has passed and tomorrow may never come. So I'll be a kid at heart and live each day as if it is my last.

"Resilience is what allows us to struggle hard and long with tragedy or loss or misfortune or change and still manage to dig deep and find our second wind. It is a kind of toughness. Each life blow no longer shatters us like a hammer hitting brick; rather it makes us stronger. It tempers us, like a hammer hitting metal. Imagine the comfort in knowing that by never giving up, by accepting the bad breaks and going on, you have lived life to the fullest and maybe will have lived it a little longer. Such peace of mind is often reward enough."

— Bill Bradley

Mr. Keith Harkins, 1997

Mr. Steve Ford

*"Three decades later, I said that boy was a better man
for how Harry touched his life."*

As a journalist reporting in both the broadcast and print media, my profession is to study, understand, and reveal what I discover to audiences I serve. Yet when it comes to life experiences, my forty-one years of observations leave me short of being qualified to pass along the treasured reward of wisdom that senior citizens gain in their journeys. Still, as the child of a father who was a professor of sociology and a mother who was an actress, I was taught early in life about the virtues of observing people — and remembering.

It is, therefore, in reflection about one person who has touched my life that I recall the strong sense of humanity that I realize we are all capable of conveying to each other. The humanity I wish to highlight is in the form of a generous regard for even the seemingly smallest of kind gestures to a child.

In marveling at the positive spirit that can be passed along in the gift of an older person's kindness to a child, I regularly recall a cherished memory of when I was just six years old. My father had hired one of his university graduate students, who supported his family by working as a carpenter, to construct an additional room on our family's home. The student, Harry Jurey, was a middle-aged man of particular modesty.

What is notable about my memories of Harry is that, from the first day that he worked to construct the addition to our home, he allowed me to follow him and ask questions throughout his daily work. It still makes me pause to recall that he never lost patience with a curious and talkative youngster's eager fascination and probably constant inquiries about his work — from his supervising the massive truck and workers in the laying of the concrete foundation for the structure, to his detailed measuring, sawing, and fabrication of the wood framing for the walls.

Mr. Steve Ford, 1998

While the memories of the series of days and weeks that I would come home from school with eager anticipation of joining Harry while he worked remain a bit hazy, there is one scene that I can remember with vivid recollection. One afternoon, Harry invited me to join him for a mid-afternoon lunch break. There I sat by his side on a bench while he opened his metal lunch box. Out came the Thermos, a hard-boiled egg, and a sandwich wrapped in wax paper. As he began to eat, I remember he paused to look down at me and then he smiled as he reached into his lunch box for one small last item, also wrapped in wax paper. It was a large, round piece of chocolate candy.

Harry opened the wax paper to reveal the chocolate dessert that apparently had been placed in the lunch box by his wife. What struck me with instant delight was that he offered the chocolate that was intended for his dessert as a joyous gesture to me. I gladly accepted the candy and promptly took a bite into the juicy morsel to discover that it was a chocolate-covered cherry. "Zowie," I thought to myself. "I've never had a chocolate-covered cherry! That's tasty!"

Harry successfully completed the addition to my family's home and years of my life seemed to quickly elapse forward from that moment in my childhood. Yet that experience remained a clear and fond memory. It wasn't until I was in my mid-thirties that it dawned on me how significant Harry's gesture was. When he gave that little six-year-old boy a chocolate cherry, he likely did not expect that child to recall the moment as an adult man more than twenty-five years later. That was the beauty, it occurred to me, of Harry's character and humanity.

Because my family remained in contact with Harry over the years, I took the opportunity to call him and his wife, Louise, one evening and asked if I could pay them a social visit. A few days later I arrived at their home and sat down with them in their living room. I proceeded to tell Harry and his wife the story about that six-year-old boy who was so flattered and excited to be given a chocolate-covered cherry by that neat guy who was a carpenter on his family's house.

Then I opened up a paper bag and pulled out a gift-wrapped box and handed it to Harry, while his amused and proud wife watched us. Harry opened the box and found that it was filled with two dozen chocolate-covered cherries. I actually became a bit emotional, as did Harry, as I explained to him that the grown man who was bringing him those chocolates was really just that grateful little boy. I told him that I never forgot his kind gesture to me, and his friendship to that curious child — a boy he could have merely brushed off, but chose to treat with sensitive kindness.

I also told Harry that the lesson in life that he showed me was a gift that demonstrated how powerful the positive effect of caring for the feelings of a child can be. Harry had treated one little boy with warmth and generosity he could have only hoped that child would appreciate, and even more remotely, remember as an adult. Three decades later, I said, that boy was a better man for how Harry touched his life.

We don't always have a chance to come back and thank those who have been kind to us. Yet perhaps more importantly, we don't always know if the children we're kind to will remember the regard we offer them. Like Harry, however, I learned that when we give to a child, it is the model for the greatest giving of all.

"The only true gift is a portion of thyself."

— Ralph Waldo Emerson

Mrs. Doris Cherry

"Live, love, listen, and forgive is my philosophy."

A very good friend of mine became estranged from her father and stopped talking to him. One day she decided to talk to me regarding this situation. She had to decide whether to leave it as it was, or try to rectify it. I had tried in the past to show her the futility of leaving it as it was, but she refused to listen.

This time I finally got through to her and convinced her that life was too short for this kind of behavior. I told her that she would feel so much better if she could just forget the past and make up with her father and forgive him for whatever it was he was supposed to have done.

It took her a little time, but she was finally able to forgive (although not forget). About six months later, her father passed away. She came to me and thanked me for giving her those last six months with her father.

Listen and don't give advice unless it is asked for. Live, love, listen, and forgive is my philosophy. We are thankful to God every day for all His blessings.

"Forgiveness is the means for taking what is broken and making it whole. It takes our broken hearts and mends them. It takes our trapped hearts and frees them. It takes our hearts blemished with shame and guilt and returns them to their unspoiled state once again. Forgiveness restores our hearts to the innocence that we once knew — an innocence that allowed us the freedom to love.

"When we forgive and are forgiven, our lives are always tranformed. The sweet promises of forgiveness are kept. And we are actually given a fresh start with ourselves and the world."

— Robin Casarjian

Mrs. Ruth Tindall

"Probably the most important lesson I learned from my mother was to accept whatever happens to me in life and make the most of it unless I can change it."

My first meaningful memories of life are during the Great Depression of the 1930s. My father died when I was three years old, leaving our mother with four daughters. I was the youngest. Dad had been a go-getter with a farm and a hired man, but Mother was a happy-go-lucky, loving, and disorganized woman. We were doomed to be poor, no matter what! In that respect, we were lucky to live during the Depression when so many others were needy, too. Probably the most important lesson I learned from my mother was to accept whatever happens to me in life and make the most of it unless I can change it.

One of my basic concerns is to please other people. When Harry and I planned to be married, we went searching for our home. After some looking, the Realtor showed us one that was fifty percent above what we were willing to pay. Jokingly I said, "Oh, this is the house I want." Harry replied, "Yes, it would be just right for us." I thought, "This is the house Harry wants, too." That is how we happened to purchase our first home. It was ten years before I learned that Harry didn't want the house either, but he thought I wanted it.

"He who wishes to secure the good of others has already secured his own."

—Confucius

Ruth and Harry Tindall, wedding portrait, 1961

Miss Marjorie Cornell

"My parents shared with others in need and this was 'passed on' to me."

My philosophy to persevere started as a child in a twenty by twenty-foot home that my father built during the Depression. It was located in the country three miles west of Ann Arbor. The fabric of my life was formed by:

- Being responsible for chores and working in the yard, garden and fields;
- Walking one mile to a one-room school through grade eight;
- Caring for my grandfather nights, arising at five a.m., walking a half mile to get a ride into Ann Arbor, walking another mile to high school, and reversing the process after school;
- Working six nights at St. Joseph's Mercy Hospital while carrying a full load of classes at the university;
- Teaching and graduating from the University of Michigan with a Master's degree were the result of persevering and reaching goals.

My parents shared with others in need and this was "passed on" to me. Besides teaching for thirty-six years, many vacations were spent sharing in Appalachia, on Indian reservations, eleven times in Haiti, and culminating with a summer of participating in youth camps around the world. Now in retirement, I find it is still a pleasure to share with others in various ways.

As other challenges have come by way of surgeries and cancer, I have sought the help of the Lord and persevered as in previous years. Each day it seems good to keep the yard beautiful, work with wood projects, or travel.

Miss Marjorie Cornell, elementary school teacher, 1990

Friends during the different periods of my life have been a blessing by encouraging, going along to share in various projects, being available in times of illness, and sharing the joys of life.

The Lord is my source of life and my source for living a fulfilling and joy-filled life.

"Perseverance opens up treasures which bring perennial joy."

— Mohandas Karamchand (Mahatma) Gandhi

Dr. Donald Mys

*". . .he proceeded to put a penny into each of my pockets
and patches on my bib overalls."*

Two characteristics come to my mind immediately when I ponder my philosophy of life. The first is fairness and the second, perseverance.

My early childhood was spent in a farming community situated in the middle of Michigan, where I attended a one-room schoolhouse from kindergarten through eighth grade. I walked the one mile to Highland Number One School each day as did my three older brothers and two older sisters. There were a total of three students in my class when I graduated!

While I was growing up, I was expected to do many tasks. I had first-hand experience hauling hay, driving tractors, assembling farm machinery, and harvesting potatoes, pickles, and green beans. Also, since my father owned the Ina General Store and an International Harvester farm-equipment dealership, I learned how to stock shelves with groceries and hardware, pump gasoline, and sell customers groceries and parts for their farm equipment. I quickly learned the rewards of working hard, serving the public fairly, and the value of earning my own money.

One memory that stays with me to this day was when my Uncle Pete from Iowa visited our family. He was considered to be our "'rich uncle" as he took each of us for a ride in his new Model A Ford. At the end of his visit he gave each one of my brothers and sisters a dollar bill. I was only five or six years old at the time, and he proceeded to put a penny into each of my pockets and patches on my bib overalls. All I received was thirteen

Dr. Donald Mys in his bib overalls, 1947

cents! I didn't think it was fair that I didn't get a dollar like all of the others. Being fair was a lesson that I never forgot and this concept has remained with me to this day.

After graduating from grade school, high school, and college, I began teaching high school mathematics at Lowrey School in Dearborn. I vividly recall the very first day of my teaching career. An unforgettable situation occurred in my first hour algebra class. I knew that I would have to make special arrangements in presenting my algebra lessons on the blackboard because I was assigned a student with a hearing impairment. This meant that whenever I was writing the math problems on the blackboard, I would have to turn toward the class and speak directly to this student because he would need to read my lips in order to comprehend. You can then imagine my dilemma when in walked another "challenged" student with a visual impairment. She was blind and unable to see the blackboard. My job then was to explain in detail every step of each math problem that I was writing on the blackboard so that the blind student could visualize it. I also had to make sure to turn toward the hearing impaired student at the same time. That semester sharpened my teaching strategies a great deal and was an unforgettable experience. But I persevered and made sure that I was fair to both of my two special students and the entire class.

My career in education included teaching at the high school, junior high school, and university levels. My administrative experience included being the Coordinator of the Testing, Research, and Evaluation Office for over twenty years and my years as an assistant principal at Fordson High School. The issue of fairness to students also comes to mind when I was responsible for the discipline of some five hundred ninth grade students. I always made sure that I gave each young adult the chance to state his or her side before a decision was made when administering the Student Code of Conduct. Being fair in what I do with my family or other people has been an important goal in my life.

When I was an assistant principal at Fordson High School, I was dealt a problem that nearly shattered my life. I suffered a heart attack that left me with one-third of my heart permanently damaged. My recovery of health has been slow but with promising progress. We have persevered with God's help.

"1. Is it the TRUTH?
2. Is it FAIR to all concerned?
3. Will it build GOODWILL and BETTER FRIENDSHIPS?
4. Will it be BENEFICIAL to all concerned?"

— The Rotary Four-Way Test

Mrs. Bette Mys

"Let's use the problems that come against us as opportunities to grow."

It's true I suffer from a chronic illness. However, my desire is to concentrate on living with the condition until a cure can be found. I am, like you, a pilgrim stumbling along the way, a common pilgrim with a common name: Bette. I wish I would be afforded healing and a cure. It would be wonderful for good health to return to my body so I could be the person I used to be. Being a loving wife to my husband, Don, and the best mother I can be to our daughters, Susan and Amy, is and will continue to be the most important thing in my life. Also, I've always tried to be a caring daughter, sister, and friend.

My profession of teaching the blind and visually impaired afforded me much joy and pleasure. My students made each day so very special and I looked forward to spending time with all of them. I still recall one of my fifth graders who was more interested in using his slate and stylus as a musical-tapping instrument instead of as a tool for brailling and completing his work assignments. This young man's name is Stevie Wonder — someone who has made quite a name for himself in the music world. Stevie always has said that I was the strictest teacher that he ever had, but the best. I demanded a lot from my students and felt strongly that their academic potentials should always be challenged and met if possible.

At the age of forty, I was accepted into law school. At this time, my chronic illness became very debilitating. It was extremely difficult for me to keep on going. An internist told me that I was overextending myself and it was imperative that I give up law school, put my real estate license in escrow, and rest. However, I kept teaching until I was virtually forced to take an extended health leave. I have never given up my extended health leave status with the schools. I feel it is something that I will keep for as long as possible because I am confident it spurs me on in my search for better health, a cure, and the ability to some-day return to teaching — my first career love.

My philosophy of life has been altered somewhat since the onset of my illness, but it remains basically the same. It revolves around love, faith, kindness, thoughtfulness, and generosity toward others. At present, it takes me longer to accomplish tasks and this often leads to much discouragement and disappointment on my part. It does, however, make me appreciate life so much more.

In the last few years, my philosophy has also been challenged by personal circumstances. It was only through prayer, counseling, and time that the situation has been resolved. Much peace within myself has occurred after I was asked by Dr. Waldinger to submit in writing some of my personal philosophical feelings toward life. Writing this statement has afforded me closure and the courage I desperately need-ed to move forward. I thank God every day for the changes that have occurred in my life, and Dr. Waldinger for asking me to contribute my thoughts for his book. It was exactly what I needed at this time in my life and it has accomplished so much more than I ever expected. I will be forever grateful to him for allowing me to be a part of his meaning-ful publication.

I believe that what people need more than anything is God, their family and their friends' love for them personally. This to me is the foundation upon which living as a Christian is formed and this can be given to an individual only through the love of God and prayer. God wants to have a personal relationship with you, but it is up to you to open up your heart to accept His love and understanding. People have a craving, a longing, and a desire in their hearts to be loved and cared about. The sun rises in the sky every day for you. When the rain comes in season, it rains for you. When the snow comes, it comes for you.

Mrs. Bette Mys (left) and sister Jean, 1948

Sometimes, I thought that people could wear God out with their failures or problems, but I learned it is impossible to do that. In January 1996, my world collapsed even more when Don suffered a massive coronary. Since that time, several other serious cardiac concerns have had to be addressed. Don lost more than one-third of his heart and has limited strength. Furthermore, the original angioplasty procedure failed and additional blockages were noted. I honestly do not think that God can be worn out or that He will ever stop loving you. Love is not something that God does, but it is who He is. He loves all people unconditionally, regardless of their problems.

We all make mistakes and have shortcomings. I will always remember when one of my daughters, who was about three or four years old at the time, was watching me do my housework. She decided one day to help me and got a little bucket of water and a rag and went to the picture window on the front porch. She scrubbed the window really well, and got a few paper towels to wipe off the window. Of course, it was all streaky, smeary, and soapy when she completed her job. She also used my best dusting cloth as her rag! She came up to me and told me that she had washed my window and did a good job. "I love you, Mommy," she said. Yes, I thanked her for helping and I did clean up the mess, but did give her some encouragement later not to do that again. As I said before, God cleans up our messes, too. You must do the best that you know how to do. However, no one expects you to do something you are not able to do.

It is impossible to rise above the image of yourself that's in your head. My problem was that I didn't like being ill and still do not and spent a great deal of time trying to change myself. When I was quiet, others thought I was depressed. I did not want to bother anyone with my health concerns. Tremendous guilt was present but I found out that no matter how guilty you feel, that is not going to help you at all. You must learn to believe that God loves you even when you feel this way. Guilt only keeps you weighed down and discouraged to the point that you cannot be free. A person must say "no" to guilt. I have learned not to feel bad about talking to others about my concerns any longer. The first few times I did this were tough, but soon I got used to it and felt so much better.

I feel that you can express your feelings to people by just sharing love, faith, and trust with them. We must all strive at having more faith, but faith of the heart can be achieved only through loving relationships. A lot of people are trying to walk in faith, but they do not have these things in their heart. Faith will not work without love.

We usually go along just fine in faith. Then all of a sudden, something attacks us. The big stealer of faith is circumstances — those bad things that happen to all of us. A person who doesn't have much trouble believes that God loves you until the circumstances make it look like He doesn't. Then you lose your confidence and it is extremely difficult to move forward. You must at this time remember that you are special and you must start to act that way and it will begin to change your life in a positive way. Love will then spread. The love you have inside you will set you free from fear, and you will not be afraid to reach out to others with love.

Nor height nor depth, nor anything else in all creation will be able to separate us from the love of God which is in Christ Jesus our Lord.

— Romans 8:39

Do not expend all of your energy concentrating on yourself and getting your own needs met. Try to simply and quickly decide what you want and then move on to meet the needs of other people. Try also to use your strength to meet every need that comes before you. The needs of others should come first. It doesn't take anything to love somebody who loves you. There is no trust in that. But when you love the unlovable, you press on and keep loving them, and you keep loving them and keep loving them.

Also, don't be afraid to step out. Be determined to spread your love around. Start by just being friendly with others. Extend your hand to others and smile. Maybe you are that special person who nobody else can reach. Letting someone know that you care and love him will make you feel good. Just take that first step and see how much it will change your life forever.

Let's use the problems that come against us as opportunities to grow. Never forget about your strong faith. If you experience love, you will be smiling all the time. Energy and strength come from loving others. Furthermore, something that Don and I have always had during extremely difficult times is a positive attitude and we are always confident that healthier and happier times are just around the corner. We also believe that God would not bestow upon us more than we could bear — although at times we did have to question God and felt we could not handle one more hardship. But, to our surprise, we knew our faith in God, the love of family and friends, and the kind and thoughtful ways of our doctors would get us through even the toughest of times. God bless you all and thank you for your caring ways. We will always hold a special place in our hearts for each and every one of you.

Is there a light at the end of the tunnel? We seem to think so, even though that light may just be a glimmer at times and not that bright and shining beam that we desire to see. We have learned that with hope and prayer we will make it in life, no matter what obstacles we might encounter along the way. Health problems are unavoidable but can be faced and challenged with the proper support team. Our life has been blessed with the kindness and caring of family, friends, and the best physicians. We are, and have been, truly fortunate to have these special individuals touch our lives so deeply and profoundly. Someone to talk to in time of need is so important and can make an unforgettable impact on a person's life.

A Gentle Breeze

The sound of your voice
The sparkle in your eyes
The bloom of a magnolia
The leaves on the trees.

The morning sun
In all its splendor
The snow-capped mountains
In their grandeur
A field of flowers
The leaves on the trees
A gentle breeze.

Search for the essence
Two souls meet
Peace, purity, faith
A friendship forever.

Close your eyes
Silent words are heard
The stars grace the sky
A field of flowers
A friendship forever.

— Thomas P. Waldinger

Part Two

Love

Love is eternal — the aspect may change, but not the essence.

— Vincent Van Gogh

Petals On A Flower

I have loved you
All of my life
Our souls together
Like petals on a flower
Like fall becomes winter
A kiss that lasts forever
All of my life
I have loved you
I have loved you.

Each new day
I feel closer to you
When our hands touch
When I hear your voice
Just the thought of you
A kiss that lasts forever
Petals on a flower
Our souls together
All of my life
I have loved you
I have loved you.

I have loved you
All of my life
Our souls together
When sadness is in our hearts
When tears are in our eyes
When the time for words has passed
Our souls together
All of my life
I have loved you
I have loved you.

You are with me
A kiss that lasts forever
Petals on a flower
Embracing faith
In the shadow
Of your wings
Petals on a flower
Precious angel
All of my life
I have loved you
I have loved you.

— Thomas P. Waldinger

Ribbon In Your Hair

Holding you in my arms
Waves of water
Rushing in my mind
Clear blue sky
Hummingbirds fly
Ribbon in your hair
I will be with you
Anywhere and everywhere
My love, my love.

Holding you in my arms
Waves of water
Rushing in my mind
Clear blue sky
Hummingbirds fly
I would only change
The days that went before
By loving you more
By loving you more
I will be with you
Anywhere and everywhere
My love, my love.

Holding you in my arms
Midnight sky
Waves of love
Rushing, rushing
Rushing in my mind
Dreams and thoughts
Become one
Faith and love

Become one
I would only change
The days that went before
By loving you more
By loving you more.

Holding you in my arms
Ribbon in your hair
I will be with you
Anywhere and everywhere
Holding you in my arms
This and this alone
Gives joy
This and this alone
Gives joy
I will be with you always
I will be with you always.

— Thomas P. Waldinger

Hand In Hand

For so many years
We have been together
Each morning kiss
Each evening embrace
Rekindles the time
We walked hand in hand
Said to each other
I am yours
You are mine.

After the rain
Peace and calm
Soft and sweet
If you listen
There is a rhythm
Soft and sweet
Peace and calm
I am yours
You are mine.

When the snow falls
And the moon is smiling
My heart is singing
I love you so
I love you so
Soft and sweet
Peace and calm
I am yours
You are mine
I love you so
I love you so.

When the sun rises
Rejoice and renewal
A chance
To begin again
If you listen
There is a rhythm
I am yours
You are mine
When your heart calls
I will be there
I am yours
You are mine.

When the rain falls
When the sun is rising
When the snow falls
When the moon is smiling
When your heart calls
I will be there
Forever, my love
My love, forever
I am yours
You are mine
My love, forever
Forever, my love.

— Thomas P. Waldinger

A Leaf In The Wind

Every time I wake
I think of your love
The moment I saw you
The way you make me feel.

You are my safe harbor
There is no other
A leaf floating in the wind
That's how we begin.

So many years ago
I looked up one day
I knew at that moment
You would be
The love of my life
The love of my life.

You are my safe harbor
There is no other
A leaf floating in the wind
That's how we begin.

You are always with me
Holding me
Comforting me
Loving me
Loving me always
Loving me when
I couldn't love myself
There is no one else.

Love of my life
Always my friend
I am born again
In your arms
A leaf floating in the wind
That's how we begin.

You are my safe harbor
You radiate love
You create joy
I am with you always.

Loving you when
You can't love yourself
There is no one else
Love of my life
Love of my life.

I am your safe harbor
There is no other
A leaf floating in the wind
That's how we begin.

Rest by my side
I will love you forever
I feel the same today
As the first moment I saw you
Love of my life
Love of my life.

— Thomas P. Waldinger

Seashells And Daffodils

Lie gently by my side
Look up in the sky
Let the trees shade your face
Let the summer breeze
Be my embrace
Lift the seashell
To your ear
You will hear
I love you, my dear
I love you, my dear.

Lie gently by my side
Let the moon shine on your face
Let the summer breeze
Be my embrace
Listen to nature's silence
Let it fill your soul
Lift the seashell
To your ear
You will hear
I love you, my dear
I love you, my dear.

Lie gently by my side
Look up to the sky
Let each star
Be my kiss
Let the summer breeze
Be my embrace
Lift the seashell
To your ear

You will hear
I love you, my dear
I love you, my dear.

Lie gently in my arms
Close your eyes
Listen to nature's silence
Let it fill your soul
Smell the daffodil
Let it fill your soul
Lift the seashell
To your ear
Forever you will hear
I love you, my dear
I love you, my dear.

Lie gently in my arms
Close your eyes
Smell the daffodil
Let it fill your soul
Feel my presence
Let it fill your soul
Lift the seashell
To your ear
Forever you will hear
I love you, my dear
I love you, my dear
For eternity
My destiny.

— Thomas P. Waldinger

Sunrise And Sunset Become One

We walk together
Even when I'm alone
I see your reflection
When I'm looking at my own.

The wind moves us together
The flowers invite us to kiss
The stars and moon become one
With you in my arms, eternal bliss.

For only you
Make my dreams come true
Soothe my soul
Illuminate my universe
The stars and moon become one
With you in my arms, eternal bliss
Only you
Only you.

I hear your voice
The wind moves us together
The world moves slowly
Sunrise and sunset become one.

For you only
Make my dreams come true
Soothe my soul
Illuminate my universe
Sunrise and sunset become one
With you in my arms, eternal bliss
Only you
Only you.

And my dream
You have made come true
Is simply my love
To live my life
With you
Only you
Only you.

— Thomas P. Waldinger

Waves A Lullaby

In your arms
No clouds in the sky
Waves a lullaby
Ocean a deep blue
Wherever I go
You come too
I love you
I love you.

In your arms
Life's fragility
Disappears gently
Waves a lullaby
Ocean a deep blue
Wherever I go
You come too
I love you
I love you.

In my heart
I felt so alone
Falling into a cocoon
In your arms
I feel so loved
Falling into my dream
Love and compassion
Delight and wisdom
Waves a lullaby
No clouds in the sky
Ocean a deep blue
Wherever I go

You come too
I love you
I love you.

So many years have gone by
Our share of joy
Our share of sorrow
Still, a sense of wonder
No clouds in the sky
Waves a lullaby
Ocean a deep blue
Trees swaying
Birds singing
Children playing
In my heart
Wherever I go
You come too
I love you
I love you.

— Thomas P. Waldinger

The Greatest Of These Is Love

By Saint Paul

Be ambitious for the higher gifts.
And I am going to show you a way
that is better than any of them.

If I have all the eloquence of men or of
angels, but speak without love, I am simply
a gong booming or a cymbal clashing.
If I have the gift of prophecy, understanding
all the mysteries there are, and knowing everything
and if I have faith in all its fullness, to move
mountains, but without love, then I am nothing at all.

If I give away all that I possess, piece by piece,
and if I even let them take my body to burn it, but
am without love, it will do me no good whatever.

Love is always patient and kind; it is never
jealous; love is never boastful or conceited; it is
never rude or selfish; it does not take offense,
and it's not resentful.

Love takes no pleasure in other people's sins
but delights in the truth; it is always ready to excuse,
to trust, to hope, and to endure whatever comes.

Love does not come to an end.

This is the word of the Lord.

Part Three

Family

*Since we are surrounded by so great a cloud of witnesses,
let us lay aside every weight, and the sin which so easily ensnares us,
and let us run with endurance the race that is set before us.*

— Hebrews 12:1

Mrs. Geraldine Robbins

"To this day, I have tears in my eyes when I remember these and other sayings of this gracious and kind woman who raised a child when she was fifty years old."

I was born an only child of a woman in the process of divorcing my father. I have never met my father. When I was born, my maternal immigrant Swedish grandma cried, "What will become of this baby?" In those early days, people with mental weaknesses, called "nerves," had no medicines to help them function successfully in society. It was 1931, and my mother wanted no part in caring for me. Her only sibling, a sister thirteen months younger, replied, "Don't cry; something good will come of this child. We will all take care of her." So began my journey in life with four caretakers: my maternal grandpa and grandma and my dear aunt and uncle.

I loved all four of my caretakers, and they were all so very good and kind to me. My aunt and uncle took me traveling with them and their only child, my cousin, a girl two and a half years younger than I. We grew up as close as sisters could have been. I spent summers with them as much as with my grandparents. I never missed the "normal" family I didn't have. It wasn't until I had a husband, two sons, and a dog of my own that I lived in a family like those I had seen as a child.

Mrs. Geraldine Robbins (right)
and her cousin, 1938

My mother was a shadow in the background. Sometimes she was able to be in society and use her teaching degree. Other times, she was back living with my grandparents and me. However, all of my values and philosophies about life were pronouncements from my dear grandma.

"Don't say anything if you don't have anything good to say." "The years go faster when you get older." "You were born so that your husband, such an ambitious and helpful person with so many talents, could help us in our old age." My husband loved my grandparents and helped Grandpa maintain many properties which he had built and rented. My husband ate my grandma's voluminous cooking with glee.

"We old people have to die off to make room for more babies to be born and have a place on this earth. That is God's plan." "Oh, I am so happy to see children eat. In the old country, we had so little to eat." (This statement might include a pinch on the cheeks of my young sons.) "Always be kind and gentle to people and animals. They all have feelings." "We don't know why your mother is the way she is. But be very quiet, and be nice to her. She can't help the way she is."

As I grew older, I was more aware of mental problems in people than any friends of mine were. I tried to understand and be kind and helpful. This ability has helped me in my own trying personal circumstances.

I was fifty-four when my first husband died in a sudden accident. He had been a loving husband and father to the three of us. We were all left with empty spaces in our lives, from which my two sons have never recovered. However, they are happy that I met a fine man and remarried after two and a half years of widowhood. He is an engineer just as their dad was, and my younger son is. They all worked in the iron and steel industry. I was also formally educated in engineering, rare for the 1950s, but dedicated my life to teaching middle school children math and science.

Grandma would say, "God has plans for our lives. We may not know what they are, but we will know when we look back." I think about her wise words often as I relive my husband's death and my meeting and marrying for a second time.

"Always be clean, dress nice, and do the best you can. We came to this country with two empty hands, and we worked from dawn to dusk to get what we have." From their examples, I learned a strong work ethic, which I applied to my education to get the best grades possible. Then I worked with diligence around my home and still enjoy every minute of that. I always thought I earned my paycheck when I was teaching school, because I used the God-given talents of creativity and ambition to create stimulating educational activities for my students.

"I need to bring food to my neighbors. They are hungry, and we are not. Help me bring this over." I have continued cooking "too much" ever since those days I helped Grandma. She taught me to knit and crochet, to bake and cook, to entertain and clean up. She taught me to help paint rooms, to sweep up messes Grandpa made as he built, and to get dirty working. No task was too much work or beneath her. Life was adventurous as you participated in the event; picking wild blueberries was a time of laughter and shared time on our knees.

To this day, I have tears in my eyes when I remember these and other sayings of this gracious and kind woman who raised a child when she was fifty years old. The Lord took her gently when she was eighty years old, with a one-week coma after a stroke. We buried her with a funeral that included a hymn so loved by the Swedes, "How Great Thou Art."

Mrs. Iva Billig

"My father worked the land and this allowed him to have
spiritual connections with God and a deep respect for all
God's creations. My mother followed the same path."

I was born May 12, 1920, in the small town of West Branch,
Michigan. My family consisted of five sisters and one brother. My
parents were farmers and did a lot of hard work for little income.
The most important factor in our lives was that my parents gave us all
a lot of love. We were able to become emotionally secure and feel a
sense of well-being. Early on in life we accepted that material things
would be scarce and we had to learn to make do and share with others.

Religion played an important role in our lives. My father worked
the land and this allowed him to have spiritual connections with God
and a deep respect for all God's creations. My mother followed the
same path. Therefore, by the example set for us by such wonderful and
devoted parents, I would like to think we grew up to be well-balanced
individuals with respect for God and our fellow man.

When it came time for high school, it was difficult for us to get to
the school without transportation being available. As a result, my parents located a good family where we could stay during the week and
work for our room and board. We were able to go home only on week-

ends. After graduating from high school, I decided to go into nursing. Looking back, I realized this wasn't so unusual. It was probably due to the example set for me by my parents. Their kindness and willingness to help all people made me realize I also wanted to help others. There is no better way to accomplish this than by being a nurse.

I'd like to relate this incident to you about how my parents were able to help someone. One day a young man approximately fifteen or sixteen years of age stopped at my parents' home and asked if he could stay the night. Of course, my parents said, "Yes." He spent the evening enjoying a good home-cooked meal and a discussion of what happened to each of us that day. The next morning he left. Thirty-five years later, when my parents were celebrating their golden wedding anniversary, they received a card in the mail. In it the writer said, "You may not remember me but I spent one night in your home and that night changed the whole course of my life. I was running away from home and the example your family set for me made me decide to turn around and go back. I now am happily married and have several children and am eternally grateful to you."

I met and married Robert Billig in 1952. We have four beautiful children: Judy, Barbara, Michael, and Jean. Throughout my life I was involved in nursing, on and off, for thirty-five years. I always enjoyed doing for others and still do. My husband died in April 1996. We were married for forty-three years. I now have another big adjustment in my life — learning to live alone. However, with my faith and trust in God and my four wonderful children, I know I will manage.

Mr. Walter Orr

*"Many years later, after I had grown up, married, and
moved away, the lesson became clear."*

I was born in a small farm town in Tennessee. I was the third of five
children and the only son of Myrtle and Leonard Orr. I guess my
life was much like other children's in our area, one of hard work,
few material things, and lots of unspoken love. Unspoken, because
both my parents were deaf-mutes. My mother and two of her sisters
were born deaf, and my father always said his deafness was caused by
a mule kick to the head when he was a four-year-old child.

One of my duties as I grew up was to accompany my father to the
general store. He would sign to me and in turn I would tell the store-
keeper what my father wanted. If the clerk needed to tell my father
something, I would listen and then sign back to my dad. As we would
be going through this procedure, people would gather around and
stare at us. I would become so embarrassed and angry that I wanted to
shout, "What are you looking at, what's wrong with you? If my dad
would just write it down, I wouldn't have to go through this!" But he
didn't; he depended on me to be his ears and his mouth. Maybe he was
embarrassed or afraid he wouldn't know what was being said to him

and he needed me, his only son, to be there. Whatever the reason, I didn't like it, but nonetheless it was a task I undertook.

Many years later, after I had grown up, married, and moved away, the lesson became clear. When I would see someone with a physical or mental handicap, I felt empathy. I didn't want to stare. I would nod my head in recognition to let them know that they had worth, that they were someone of value. The lesson I had learned in the old country store was one of compassion. A lesson learned from a silent, gentle father.

Walter and Violet Orr, newly married,
and his parents, 1943

Mrs. Sara Montemurri

"It is a coincidence that both my cousin and mother
shared the same birthday — November 11."

My mother, Grace Montemurri (née Caruso), was born on November 18, 1905, in Detroit. She was one of nine children born to Joseph and Angeline Caruso. On December 2, 1922, at the age of seventeen, she married my father, Angelo Montemurri, a marriage that lasted over fifty years. The Depression years were a struggle, but they survived the hardships with Mother taking in boarders to help out financially. She cooked, cleaned, washed clothes by hand, and did the ironing. She thought nothing of washing walls, shoveling snow, and cutting the grass. She did whatever needed to be done.

In spite of her great strength and spirit and all the hardships she endured, she was extremely nervous when she first went to see Dr. Waldinger. However, his caring and soothing manner soon put her at ease. In subsequent visits, she was much less apprehensive.

She led a caring, giving life and her greatest joy was her family. Nothing was too much to do for them. When she reached the age of eighty-six, she was diagnosed with renal failure and given six weeks to live. My brother and I took care of her at home for a while, but then decided that it would be better for her to go to a hospice facility. She surprised everyone and survived for eight months thanks to the wonderful care she received. While there, she was a favorite with all the staff, always cheerful, giving advice and sharing her recipes. She was a wonderful Italian cook with everything homemade, including bread and pasta.

On September 12, 1994, she passed away, beloved by all her family and friends. When I called my cousin in Syracuse, New York, she immediately made plans to attend the funeral. It is a coincidence that both my cousin and mother shared the same birthday — November 11. However, the next morning my cousin injured her knee and had to be taken to the hospital for surgery. Mother's funeral was the same day as her surgery. My cousin was nervous about the surgery and upset that she could not be with us for the funeral. However, as my cousin was being wheeled into the operating room, a nurse came to her and held her hand. She said, "My name is Grace. Don't be afraid. We'll take good care of you." My cousin was comforted and knew that Aunt Grace was taking care of her family, looking down from heaven.

Mrs. Sara Montemurri and great-granddaughter, Lauren, 1990

Mr. & Mrs. Robert Briggs

*"They were born and raised on an island and
rest to eternity on an island."*

One month in 1955 I interviewed on tape my mother and dad, my grandfather (Edward Neusesser) and Jennie's folks (Christine and David Bruce) to get their life stories. I conducted the interviews to satisfy my curiosity about a way of life that was fading from their memories. The interview with Jennie's parents was particularly interesting.

At first Christine was reluctant to talk about the past, preferring to "let sleeping dogs lie," so to speak. But as David told stories and answered questions, she got caught up in the spirit of the interview and became quite loquacious. At the end, she recovered her taciturn character and indignantly asked, "Why are we telling you all these things?"

I didn't respond but rewound the tape and said, "Now I'm going to play it back and you can listen to everything you said." That was particularly interesting because they had never before heard the sound of their own voices on tape. They sat enthralled and I didn't have to delete a word. Jennie was astounded at their answers because she heard things about the old country, their families, and their lives that she had never heard before.

Jennie and Bob Briggs, sixtieth wedding anniversary, Thanksgiving 1998

Years later I sat down with a recorder and computer to reduce the interviews to hard copy. I was shocked to realize that thirty years had passed since I made the recordings. Our folks had all passed away and there were their voices speaking to me once again.

When Jennie and I listen to the old recordings or read what they said, we are fascinated more by how their lives have influenced ours than by the technological changes and improved standard of living that had occurred during theirs.

Without being aware of it, Jennie and I modeled our lives after theirs — marriage, a family, dedication to each other, family survival through the trials and tribulations of wars, depressions, and illness.

Being with each other, having fun together, seeing our progenies give rise to more progenies, and then recognizing that they are our immortality.

Jennie and I respectfully submit brief stories and anecdotes that will serve to give you some glimpse of our parents, their lives, and how they influenced ours. It is a pleasure having this opportunity to reminisce and once again reaffirm the importance of our parents in our lives.

A Brief History of the Parents of Janet (always Jennie) and Robert (always Bob) Briggs

Jennie's maternal grandmother, Janet Wilson of Scotland, married Arthur Cowan in 1876 and had ten children, seven boys and three girls. Jennie's mother, Christine, the eldest girl, became a second mother to the family. Arthur died in 1906.

Jennie's paternal grandmother, Isabella of Scotland, married James Bruce in 1880 and had three boys. Jennie's father, David Bruce, the eldest boy, was thirteen years old when his father died. As a means of providing family income, David was indentured for seven years to a brass manufacturing company to become a journeyman.

Christine lived in Airdrie, Scotland, and David lived a short distance away. David knew one of Christine's brothers but didn't know her. One day he saw him talking to her and later on asked if he knew the girl. The brother responded with, "Well, I ought to. She's my sister." Of course, they were introduced and from that time on they were always "Teen and David."

Still teenagers, it wasn't long before they were making plans for their future. It was agreed that David would complete his training, become a journeyman, and go to America where he would work and save money to send for Teen.

The seven years completed, David was called into the office where he was presented his journeyman papers and told to report to the plant the next morning at the full pay of one pound per day. David accepted his papers, politely thanked them and said, "I won't be reporting to the plant because I'll be sailing to America on the *Sicilian*." He spent ten days in steerage where he had a wonderful adventure and good food, and landed in Halifax, Canada, in 1906.

He worked wherever jobs took him in Canada and the States, and in 1910 he sent for Christine. She sailed first class to America on the *Columbia* and landed in New York City. They were married the next day in Nyack. Ultimately they settled in Detroit, Michigan, where David worked at the Cadillac Motor Car Company. Christine's mother, five brothers, both sisters, and many friends emigrated from Scotland and stayed with the Bruces until they found housing of their own. David's mother immigrated to Hamilton, Canada, where she stayed with friends. She occasionally visited David and Christine, but Canada was always home to her.

A Briggs from England arrived in America in 1680 and settled in Rhode Island. In 1776, five of the Briggs family served in the American Revolutionary Army. When it was over, Joseph Briggs went west and settled in Windsor, Ohio, where my grandfather, Alfred Briggs, was born. He served four years with the Third Ohio Infantry Regiment in the Civil War and was discharged in 1865. He met and married my grandmother, Lydia, in Lansing, Michigan. They had two boys, Harry (my father) and Bernard. Grandfather Alfred died in 1902 and the boys were placed in a Grand Army of the Republic orphanage in Dayton, Ohio, where they lived until they completed high school.

Jennie was fourteen years old and I was fifteen when we met at Woodland Beach, Michigan, on Lake Erie, where our folks had summer cottages. From that summer on, it was always "Jennie and Bob." Jennie went to commercial college and worked while I went to Michigan State University. We married after I graduated as a civil engineer and followed projects around the country, eventually returning to Wyandotte, Michigan, and then Grosse Ile.

Our parents retired to Florida but occasionally returned to Michigan for brief visits. One summer when Jennie's folks were visiting us in Wyandotte, we were sitting in the back yard with our Scotty dog, and David became annoyed at noisy children playing in the alley. He got up, went back, and shouted over the fence for them to be quiet, then came back and sat down. Jennie's mother looked at him and said, "David, why do we have a dog if you're going to do all the barking?"

I stifled my laughter while David looked at me with sparkles in his eyes and said, "She is always saying things like that to me."

Until that moment I hadn't realized what a remarkable woman Christine was — intelligent, kind, quiet, reticent to speak up against anyone, never gossiped, had a wonderful sense of humor, and was generous to a fault. If there ever was a real Pollyanna, Christine Bruce was one. Everyone liked her, especially children — she was an ideal mother-in-law and grandmother.

When our children visited Grandma, the first thing they'd say was, "Make us a cake, Grandma," and she did. She never used a recipe and never a spoon. The children watched in fascination as she shook in flour, a gob of butter, little of this, a dob of that, a shake of salt, pinches of various materials, and finally a splash of milk. With the bowl in her lap she mixed the ingredients with vigor using the first two fingers of her right hand.

While the cake was baking, she made frosting the same way. That's when the children ran for slices of bread on which she spread gobs of frosting — with the first two fingers of her right hand. The diminished ingredients were replaced using the "little of this and that" technique. Her cakes and frostings were delicious.

It was said that back in Scotland, she read aloud to the family and she did the same in America to visiting sisters, brothers, and families. One of our children once asked if she could draw a map of the United States. She proceeded to make a free-hand sketch, adding the states and their names.

Christine had the gift of perspicacity and could analyze a situation before you realized there was a problem. One time Jennie and I went shopping with her and the clerk was downright ornery and offensive. Christine said to the woman, "My-y-y, you must be having a bad day."

The clerk stopped what she was doing, looked at Mom for an instant, and tears flowed down her cheeks. Her voice trembled as she said, "Oh-h-h I have! Everything has gone wrong today and you're the first person who understood." She dried her eyes with a tissue and said, "I feel better all ready." That was Christine — she always made you feel better.

After happy years in Florida, Christine and David became too old to live alone and Jennie and I brought them home to live with us on Grosse Ile. We lived together in gentle harmony and what we did, they did. They enjoyed having me play hymns on the organ and quietly sang or hummed along. Jennie often cooked dinners using Mom's recipes that originated in Scotland. One was called "mintz" and consisted of ground meat and chopped onions, topped with sliced potatoes and simmered in a frying pan. It was popular back in Scotland because it was inexpensive and simple to prepare — important when cooking for a family of twelve.

Jennie spiced it up, added a few more ingredients and created a delicious dinner. One time we had mintz and were having coffee and cake afterward when Pa told Jennie how much he'd enjoyed the mintz. I said, "You know, Mom, whenever I came home from college for a visit, you always served mintz." Mom kind of glowed at the recollection. Then I added, "But, you know, I didn't like it very much because it was so bland."

Right out of the blue, without thinking, David spoke up and said, "Neither did I."

Mom was absolutely flabbergasted and said, "Why, I thought you liked it."

Pa knew he had blundered and didn't know what to say so he stood up, said, "Naw," and walked out of the room. Mom sat speechless, feeling hurt I'm sure, but typically didn't make an issue of it.

Consider: Mom had cooked mintz for Dave all their married life because she thought he liked it. Pa had eaten it all those years without complaining because he didn't want to hurt her feelings. That is true love.

David died three years before Christine. Both were eighty-nine years old. They were cremated and laid to rest in the Memorial Garden of the Grosse Ile Presbyterian Church. They were born and raised on an island and rest to eternity on an island.

Epilogue

The Book of Genesis in the Old Testament describes the creation of man in God's image. It tells that man was created from dust and placed in the Garden of Eden. God named the animals and then discovered he hadn't created a fitting mate for man and formed Eve from his rib.

The religion of the ancient Greeks describes a similar creation but a different version. God created man but not woman. God became so exasperated at man's outrageous acts that he cleaved man into two halves, thus creating man and woman. Ancient Greek philosophers believed this story and said that was why men and women were ever searching the world for their matching halves.

Christine and David Bruce
Elsie and Harry Briggs

They were abidingly faithful to each other, fully aware of their own strengths, weaknesses and peculiarities and those of their mates, and accepted each other without hesitation or reluctance.

The matching halves were joined and became one, and became role models for their progenies.

Mrs. Lucienne Gosselin

*"Up until then, she was still knitting sweaters for
needy children all over the world."*

I was born in Thetford-Mines, Quebec, and moved to the United
States with my husband and three children when I was thirty-four
years old. Perhaps the one person who taught me the most and had
the strongest influence on my life was the woman who raised me,
Caroline Perreault. I had three older brothers and an older sister. My
mother died giving birth to me, so I never knew her. The woman I
think of as "mother" came into my life after having suffered as many
tests and setbacks as a human could be expected to endure.

Mother had been married at a young age and was widowed after
ten years. She moved to the U.S. and worked in a shoe box factory in
Manchester, New Hampshire, for the next several years. One day she
received a request from the sister of her deceased husband. This poor
woman, pregnant with her ninth child, had just become a widow herself. Her husband died in a mining accident. Caroline didn't hesitate.
She went back to Quebec immediately to help. Her sister-in-law then
died and Caroline ended up caring for these children for the next two
years.

My father, having been a widower for two years, asked Caroline to marry him and she agreed. Then she had two children with my father and I now had two younger sisters.

Mother was very wise. She was from the "spare the rod, spoil the child" school of child raising. Whenever one of us kids did something wrong, Mother would wait until we went to bed before telling Father about it. That way, he usually didn't hand out such a strict punishment. A good night's rest tempered his response to the transgression.

She and Father were married for sixteen years before he died of tuberculosis. Again, this woman found herself a widow raising seven children. She taught us many things — the most important of all being loving and caring for others. The woman I knew as "mother" was with us until she died at the age of ninety-five. Up until then, she was still knitting sweaters for needy children all over the world.

Mrs. Lucienne Gosselin and her mother, Mrs. Caroline Perreault,
Quebec City, 1970

Mrs. Georgia Joseph

"My eyes, come and take me."

My birthplace was Bay City, Michigan. I am of Greek and Lebanese descent and the second oldest of five girls. We were raised with love by very strict parents. Religion was very important and I feel that is the reason I have such strong religious beliefs today. It was necessary for me to leave school in the ninth grade to work in my father's restaurant. I also did ironing for people and helped to care for my grandparents, who spoke no English. This enabled me to speak fluent Lebanese.

My grandfather and two of his sons were blind. Their blindness was due to a hereditary eye disease. It is interesting to note that my mother was blind for approximately six months. She, however, sought treatment at the University of Michigan Medical Center and her sight was restored.

Our family resided with my blind grandfather. He had partial vision at one time, but because he refused to go for diagnosis and appropriate medical care, he eventually lost all of his vision. My grandfather had been a mason in Lebanon, and in America he owned his own lumberyard. He was extremely independent and could easily move around his workplace accomplishing the tasks that needed to be done.

It was very difficult for me to understand my grandfather's blindness. I strongly felt that if he was able to do so many things while blind, anyone could do anything. His favorite saying to me was, "My eyes, come and take me." If he heard a person rattling a can for money, he immediately asked me to take a dollar from his pocket and deposit it in the can. He would do the same for all jingling cans of beggars he heard on the streets.

People often would ask what was wrong with my grandfather and I would respond by saying, "He's blind and cannot see." Their stares never bothered my grandfather but they surely made me more tolerant of challenged people. My grandfather thought that he was just the same as everyone else and his handicap was not an issue.

I feel that I was my grandfather's "eyes." If you truly care for someone, anything can be accomplished in life. I have great empathy for

Mrs. Georgia Joseph (center), her parents and siblings, 1921

blind people because I feel they have missed so much because they can-not see. My grandfather, however, never complained of his blindness. He totally accepted his disability. God gave him a certain talent to do so many things and my grandfather was a living example of this.

I originally came to Detroit to help my sister. It was here that I met my husband, who also came from a loving family. We both tried to instill in our children the importance of family ties, hard work, and belief in God. I feel that these things are the keys to success. A person must not be afraid to get his hands dirty and must accept what life deals him. One must go forward and accept life's ups and downs. My eightieth birthday was celebrated this year.

Mrs. Georgia Joseph, seventy-fifth birthday celebration,
October 14, 1993

Mrs. Flora Gorman

*"If I do nearly as well as they did, the Lord will be well
pleased with me, too."*

I was born sixty-five years ago in a tiny Italian village about ninety
miles south of Rome. Although I lived there only two years, that
community, its culture and ethnicity shaped my life and greatly
influenced every aspect of the person I am today.

The little village, named Pietrafita, could not support all of its
families, few as they were. My parents, brother, two sisters and I lived
with our paternal grandparents on their farm. I am the youngest of the
four children, sixteen years younger than my brother, and fourteen and
twelve years younger than my sisters, respectively. Grandpa's land provided only enough food to feed our household. During a good year, a
few crops might bring in just enough money to buy fabric for our mea-
ger clothes, and perhaps enough for one pair of shoes for the two or
three lucky family members who needed them most. (My husband
says that explains what he calls my "shoe fetish.")

It was clear to my dad, long before I was born, that he could not
provide the kind of life he wanted for his family in Italy. He began
then to seek his fortune in Rome, Spain, England, and the United
States of America.

After many trips back to Italy, he finally convinced my mother that America offered the best opportunity for a better life for all of us. She was naturally reluctant, being forty-five years old at the time, and having to leave her mother, relatives, friends and the only culture and language she knew.

In October 1935, when I was two years old, we left for America. Certainly 1935 was not a good year in any city in the United States. There were hard times, many hard years, but Dad, having survived the union wars at the Ford Motor Company in Dearborn, was able to seek out a life that was ultimately better than what we had in our little Italian village.

My parents' work ethic rubbed off on all of us children. We all worked hard at whatever we did. My sisters married at the tender ages of seventeen and eighteen, disappointing my parents by not getting a higher education, but pleasing them by working very hard at being good spouses, parents, and homemakers. My brother also disappointed them by not going to college, but they were very proud of him when he became one of the vice-presidents of a major auto parts company.

I achieved a Master's Degree in Elementary Education and it was a great source of pride for my parents and for me. I'm delighted that they lived to see my two sons and several of my siblings' children receive college diplomas. That was the fulfillment of the American dream they had for their family.

At Mom and Dad's funerals, the eulogist said, "He (She) fought the good fight, ran the race, and it is finished. In him (her), I know the Lord is well pleased." I thank them every day for having the courage to pull up their roots and travel to a new country, and for all the sacrifices that entailed, in order to give us an opportunity for a better life.

I thank God for the gift of having had two such loving parents and for all the blessings He has bestowed on me and my loved ones. Every day I can see something of my parents in my thoughts, actions, and behaviors, and in those of my sons, Mark and Bill, and even in those of my five grandchildren. Mom and Dad taught me, by example, how to walk in the ways of the Lord and I'm trying to do the same for my family. If I do nearly as well as they did, the Lord will be well pleased with me, too.

Mrs. Harriet Sawyer

"I will be with you always."

A
fter only twelve years of marriage, my minister husband died
suddenly, leaving me to raise three children alone. When my
mind and emotions cleared, I realized we would have to find
a place to live because we were living in the church parsonage at that
time. I also knew I needed surgery in the near future. The last straw
broke when our eldest child fell from the monkey bars at school, frac-
tured his upper arm, and had to spend a month in traction at
Children's Hospital. "Dear God," I cried. "This is more than I can
handle. Too many needs! Not a clue, no direction!"

I had always been independent, even in childhood. My mother
died when I was only fifteen and my dad and I had managed alone,
leaving me pretty much on my own through high school and part of
my college days. This was different, I thought. I was devastated and
desperate. I had forgotten the strength of family and friends. "First
things first," one of them said. Our first break came when an acquain-
tance stopped by, offering to help us find a new place to live. Together
we located a cozy house in Dearborn and it was just a perfect size. We
moved in the week before Christmas and it became our home for forty
years.

My firstborn child entered the first grade and I had surgery that same spring. The following fall, number two entered kindergarten. At about the same time, I was offered a part-time position in an area of interest to me. It turned into a full-time position and I stayed at the same job for fifteen years. But what about the baby? Before I accepted the position, a kind and caring lady literally appeared on our doorstep and became a substitute mother and housekeeper for our family. How lucky could we be? She grew so attached to us

Mrs. Harriett Sawyer, 1996

that she continued to stay with us off and on until the children finished high school and then college. She even attended one of their weddings!

During the children's early years, I occasionally talked to them about their father, reminding them of things he had said and done. This was to help them remember him and, in the beginning, to aid in their grief. "Do you think he knows what's happening to us?" the oldest asked. I replied that I was sure of an awareness, because Dad's love was strong — it was eternal. Then I read them the engraved message inside my wedding ring: "I will be with you always." It had been close to me for many of the past difficult years.

The children are grown now with children of their own and I am finding how great it is to be a grandparent. Recently, one of the college-aged grandsons was telling me about a girl he had met in school. He is very much in love and hopes someday to marry her. Then he asked about his granddad and me. I showed him the well-worn band on my finger. He was thrilled to be able to make out the lettering: "I will be with you always."

Suddenly I had a flash of insight. That was it. The message on the ring was not my husband's alone. They are the final words of Jesus at the end of the book of St. Matthew when He says, "For lo, I will be with you always, even until the end of the world!"

How wonderful life can be!

Mrs. Margaret Parsons

*"At an early age, I learned to appreciate
the simple details in our home."*

Reflecting on my life brings back many occasions and situations that I truly feel influenced my personal beliefs and attitudes. These experiences helped to develop my way of life and also assisted my children in their ability to make better decisions.

I grew up during the Depression, when the banks crashed and everyone had to delve within themselves for resources to continue living. My parents were born into pioneering families, facing numerous challenges to exist. They were both from large families who had learned to share resources and responsibilities within their own households and, indeed, experienced many unique lessons.

At an early age, I learned to appreciate the simple details in our home. My mother used to let us watch her when she baked bread or when she prepared a cake or cookies for some very special occasion, because she had to save sugar, only using it sparingly. She always saved bits of dough or ingredients for us to blend in our projects, relating stories of the grains they used to raise and have ground for flour. She sometimes shared with the Indians who would stop and ask for flour.

Mrs. Margaret Parsons, 1997

She taught us to observe textures of each food to gauge the finished product.

My father used to entertain us in the evening before bedtime with stories he had heard and many experiences of his own youth, always with something we could glean for our own practical knowledge. He had a great repertoire of songs and stories. We felt blessed with knowledge and entertainment.

My parents had great faith in God and faithfully took us to church. We had few material things, yet felt blessed and enriched for the sharing of knowledge and love. I believe my children benefited from my background and learned to accept what we couldn't change, but appreciate what we did have.

When my children were very young, their father became critically ill and we had many years of severe circumstances to accept. The children bravely accepted it all, and had to help raise each other when their father did pass away. We value each other.

Mrs. Margaret Vanderwill

"Grandma was a gem — not only for her courage in dealing with difficulties and hardships, but for her love of life and all people."

My philosophy of life was greatly influenced by my maternal grandmother. She was a most loving and compassionate person. She had a very meaningful life filled with incredible challenges, grief, and joy.

My grandmother inspired me for my entire life. When I was approximately eight years old, she began to introduce me to the beautiful things in the world. Her lovely manners, grace, and ability to celebrate the happy experiences in life were remarkable.

I recall a very special occasion when we went to a tea at the Henry Ford mansion. My memories are so vivid that I can still see Mrs. Ford serving tea from a lovely teapot. The petite tea sandwiches and exquisite little tea cookies were delicious. The massive table was covered with an elegant lace cloth. I was so impressed. As I reflect back, I feel that this charming event inspired my love for beautiful things and happy times.

However, my remarkable grandmother had another side to her dynamic personality. She was so kind to the poor and the sick. Her example taught me that I could be a complete person and experience the full spectrum of life's offerings. Grandma inspired me to enjoy it all and live a life filled with meaning and purpose.

During the Depression, Grandma would work all day in her own home helping individuals find work, getting clothes for their children, and assisting them in keeping their bills paid. In fact, she became one of the first registered social workers in western Wayne County.

After a hard day's work and no compensation, Grandma would pick me up and drive to the St. Joseph's Retreat at Michigan Avenue and Outer Drive. She would get pans of hot soup and homemade bread from the Sisters of Charity and deliver food to the poor residing in the outskirts of Dearborn. This act of kindness would occur after 7:30 p.m. when the patients at the Retreat were all fed and leftovers were available.

Grandma was a gem — not only for her courage in dealing with difficulties and hardships, but for her love of life and all people. Color or religion did not matter to this exceptional woman. She felt that each individual was a valuable human being.

Her mission and vision certainly influenced my life. I became a registered nurse and strived to emulate her. Her profound ability to balance human service along with enjoying the beauty of everyday life has always inspired me. Grandma taught me to be the best I could be, to care deeply for all people and their enduring issues, and that inner strength is a gift of faith.

❧

Mrs. Margaret Vanderwill's grandmother,
Mary K. Moody Buckenberger, 1895

Mrs. Milka Puroff

"I think that in order to have a meaningful life, one needs to have others to give to and be needed by, as well as to lean on for support."

I was born in Toledo, Ohio, on November 22, 1928. We were raised in a very tightly knit immigrant community on the east side of the city. My father, a self-made businessman, made sure we had the best of everything. Because of his distrust of banking institutions, we were never touched by the financial plights of other families during the Depression.

We traveled abroad, took dance and horseback riding lessons, and our mother saw to it that we (the girls) were proficient as cooks and housekeepers. All in all, we were a typical first-generation 1930s family of comfortable means.

Not surprisingly, my feelings on the important things in life also center around the family. I was raised to become a dutiful daughter, wife, and mother, and to this end I have given it my utmost. I married at age twenty-six and raised three daughters, all successful and accomplished young women. I believe helping my children is and always will be my first priority in life. My most important aspect of existence is my family. After losing my husband to cancer, my friendships with others, especially other widows, have deepened and developed into a

Mrs. Milka Puroff as child with aunts and mother, Greece, 1932

(as my daughters jokingly refer to it) "Widow Brigade." We have so much in common and it's a comfort to know I can talk to and relate to someone who shares the feelings and situations widowed senior citizens are faced with in daily life.

My church and community work are third in my hierarchy of importance in my life. To this I commit many hours in the capacity of church board member as well as president of my seniors club.

I think that in order to have a meaningful life, one needs to have others to give to and be needed by, as well as to lean on for support. Without the love and support of family and friends, one's life would be sad, empty, and meaningless. The give and take of family and friendships is, in my opinion, what a fulfilling life is all about.

Mrs. Amelia Rutila

"I loved every day of it."

The greatest influence in my life was my parents. They were Finnish immigrants who came to America to better their lives. My father came here at the age of seventeen, because he would have otherwise been taken into the Russian Army. I wish I knew more about his life and his coming to Canada and then moving to the Upper Peninsula of Michigan. He worked in the copper mines and eventually became a farmer. After farming, he became an insurance agent.

In the meantime, he learned the English language with the help of my sisters and brothers. He believed so strongly in education that it was instilled in all of us. I remember when my oldest sister came home, books and all, and said she quit school. She knew better, though, because she went back the next day, finished high school, and became a teacher, like my three other sisters and I.

Mother came to America as an indentured servant. She had worked for a Lutheran minister who paid her way so she could come to this country. She was a quiet soul who believed in helping those in need. I remember when we had a terrible flu epidemic in this country. Homes were quarantined and families were in desperate need of help

Mrs. Amelia Rutila, 1924

and food. Mother was always ready to help. She waited until the dark of night before she would go to help her neighbors with food and home-made loaves of bread. We as children worried that she might be seen and would be reported to the authorities. She always said, "You can't let human beings suffer."

It was a coincidence that my first teaching job was in the south end of Dearborn at the Salina School. My students were immigrants whose parents came from many European countries. I couldn't begin to name all the nationalities because there were so many. I guess my own background helped these children with their difficulties. It was rewarding for me to spend thirty-eight years in the same school. Education was so important to these students, like mine had been in the far north of Michigan.

Having had so many experiences, I'll just mention what happened to me a few weeks ago. I was in the grocery store and this woman came up to me and said, "You are Mrs. Rutila. Do you remember me?" I had to look closely at her and then a bell rang. "You are Lena Carpalango." Lena had won a spelling bee one Friday. We had a spelling bee every Friday. The students knew I would always reward them with something. She got a Hershey bar and was so delighted because she had never had a candy bar. She came from a family of twelve. Most of the families in the area were large, and they had very little.

Another student heard I was at the Salina School's seventy-fifth anniversary. She wrote to me from Florida and reminded me that she still had the dictionary that she received after winning a spelling bee. Some time I will tell you about the doctor I met who recognized me. I taught him in the third grade in 1939.

Teaching was my mission in life. What more can I say, at the age of ninety-two? I loved every day of it.

Mrs. Betty Szekely

*"Don't complain, and remember you can do anything
if you sincerely try."*

By the examples my father gave me to follow and his explana-
tions of how to adjust to problems, my moral and religious values and attitudes were formed. My father helped me to adjust
smoothly to the outside world. He inculcated in me two ideas that
have helped me through life: Don't complain, and remember you can
do anything if you sincerely try.

My father and I spent a great deal of time together fishing. His
insightful discussions with me as we sat in the rowboat were more
meaningful than any sociology or psychology class that I was ever
enrolled in. Early on, he taught me how to mediate disputes with my
parents, peers, relatives, and neighbors. By example, I was shown that
there are other alternatives in all disputes. It is a waste of time to blame
others for our problems. In other words, don't complain. Many con-
flicts in our lives could be brought to a quick conclusion if we would
search our hearts for alternatives and not be prideful. Instead of complaining, my father told me that if I tried to be kind, cheerful, and
considerate to others, my heart would be able to handle life's catastro-
phes. During his life, he showed me daily these qualities and they

always seemed to work for him, thus the more reason for me to emulate him.

Because it was always his suggestion that I could succeed in any endeavor if I tried, after staying home and raising my two sons, I began college at the age of forty. Never did it occur to me that I couldn't do it. My goal was a college degree from the University of Michigan. I shared this goal through the years during office visits with Dr. Ulrich. He also supported my goal. In fact, Dr. Ulrich and my father were both tremendous counselors. How frightened I was that first day of college, yet I never doubted that I could do it. Three years later, I received my degree from the University of Michigan, proof you can reach your goals if you sincerely try.

Recently, I found a wall plaque with the following verse:

"Lord, help me remember that nothing is going to happen today that YOU and I can't handle."

The teachings of my father, the love of my Lord, and the above verse get me through each day. What a great and wondrous life I have had.

Mr. Earl Lewis

"When my three children were growing up, I made it a point never to be too busy to answer their questions."

I was born in Cumberland, Maryland, in August 1922. This is a small city in western Maryland in rather a scenic, mountainous country. I was an only child but had lots of cousins.

In 1942, I enlisted in the U.S. Army and was in the southwest Pacific Operations, namely New Guinea and the Philippine campaigns from October 1942 to October 1945. It was then when I realized how important life is, especially with death hovering all around.

I suppose it was through these experiences that I decided I was going to have an attitude of, "It is better to be nice to people. A smile or a pleasant word is not that difficult."

When my three children were growing up, I made it a point never to be too busy to answer their questions. If I did not know the answer, I would search around until I did. I remember one time a group of us were at a friend's house talking and socializing, when his youngest son ran in the room and tried to get his dad's attention. Well, the father ignored the son and sent him away. Shortly after that, his oldest son came in the room and told his dad that a room in the house was on fire! If the father had listened, the damage would not have been nearly as bad.

My wife, Jacqueline, was terminally ill with lung and bone cancer in the early 1990s. This lady suffered terribly, but never complained. Then one night she said, "I wish I would go to sleep and never wake up." That was her gentle way of saying, "I have had enough." She was more concerned about me attending to her than her problem.

Mr. Earl Lewis, 1980

Mrs. Jan Smith

"Life presents many challenges, but it also equips us to meet them."

I have long believed that how we choose to interact with the people we live and work with, meet on a daily basis, or maybe meet just once in a lifetime, is fundamental to how we experience life. Right now, with family activities and commitments being what they are, I find I do not always take much time to write down my thoughts about life. As my mother, who is in her late eighties, points out, one day later on in life there may well be too much free time again, and I will cherish the memories of these busy times, wishing I had some of those same things to fill my days.

I consider it a true blessing to have had a close, supportive family. My parents have always demonstrated their love, concern, and generosity to their three daughters and their families. Beginning as a child, in fact, I was naively puzzled when I began to notice that not all siblings were as fortunate as we sisters were to share a closeness that transcended a twelve-year age difference from youngest to oldest and many geographical separations over the years. Often my sisters and I joke that we share a mental, almost telepathic bond. Why did I feel the urge years ago to interrupt a vacation in Berchtesgaden, Germany, to return to my home in Mainz to find the telegram announcing my nephew's birth? Something drew me home, and perhaps it was nothing more than coincidence. However, I often feel drawn to contact my sisters and mother without realizing what it is that's calling us together, only to discover that they have had a similar feeling.

This close family bond, also enjoyed with my father when he was alive, has helped me learn about love, spirituality, compassion, loyalty, humor, sadness, hard work, and a host of other aspects of life and the human condition. My family has always been there as I've dealt with whatever life has brought me, and it's given me an awareness of how to savor that which is good in people and learn from those around us. Life's lessons come in the most unexpected places and from the most unexpected events, desired or undesired. There is always something to learn from what life presents and growth comes from learning to deal with whatever comes your way without losing faith.

At times of a parent's or young nephew's death, the prolonged pain and illness of a dear one, depression suffered by a loved one, miscarriages, separations, unkindness, anger, and despair, the challenge is always to remain steady, strong, and focused on constants, such as religious beliefs. My father always reminded me "this too shall pass." These are all parts of life.

The examples of behavior modeled in my parents' love, respect for each other, strength of character, and integrity are still inspirational to me. Throughout his more than fifty years in banking, starting ironically enough at the time of the Great Depression, my father always showed a keen interest in people and his dealings with them were permeated with kindness and respect. I feel they sensed his genuine interest in them and their concerns and responded positively to that.

As a wife and parent myself, I hope I am sharing with my husband and daughters the essence of what I feel I was fortunate to learn at home. Both my husband, David, and I realize and appreciate what an awesome responsibility it is to be a parent. I may not have thought much at the time about hearing at home, "We love you," "You're doing great," "Keep up the good work," "Give it your best," "You can do it,"

Mrs. Jan Smith (center) and her sisters, Gretchen and Kathryn, 1949

and "The Lord never gives you any challenge you can't handle." Now I realize how much encouragement and faith can do.

It couldn't have been easy for my parents to watch me go to Germany to study and work when I wasn't yet twenty-one. Their support allowed me the opportunity to pursue a field of study I love and let me experience what it's like to make your way in another culture using a foreign language. That experience definitely shapes my thinking still and provides me coping skills to this day. Those skills certainly were of help as my husband and I relocated numerous times, far from family, during his career as an Army officer. Whenever we went to a new location, we always made a home and were blessed to connect with many wonderful people. We did have too many goodbyes to say, but also learned to realize and enjoy what each new location presented us. Kindness received often couldn't be returned directly to the givers because they had moved on, but we learned to be grateful and pass on the good deed to someone else, even if in another place and time.

Life presents many challenges, but it also equips us to meet them. The joy in doing so comes from our faith, our attitude, our initiative, and our responses to people and things around us. My final thought is that life is a precious gift to be appreciated and used as it was intended. It is worth one's best efforts; we never know where some small, seemingly inconsequential deed or happening can lead. That's the challenge and fun of seeing where the journey leads.

As a parting thought, I'm including a portion of one of my favorite closings from our worship services at church:

"Go out into the world in peace;
have courage;
hold on to what is good;
return no one evil for evil;
strengthen the fainthearted;
support the weak, help the suffering;
honor all people;
love and serve the Lord,
rejoicing in the power of the Holy Spirit."

Mrs. Bernice Ash

"At my age life is drawing its curtain on me,
but every day seems sweeter."

My father's mother, my grandmother, must have been the guiding light in my life. She was blind for twenty-five years, and yet she learned the Bible by heart and became an ordained minister. Every summer she would come on the train, a three-day journey, to stay with us for the entire summer. All three children had to walk her to church every Sunday. It was a long walk and we had to watch very carefully that she did not stumble and fall. Every bump in the sidewalk had to be avoided. We really felt very important after we had arrived safely at the church and then again back home. She must have had great faith to be guided by three young children. I was the oldest at nine years of age.

Right before going to bed, she would tell us wonderful stories from the Bible about Joseph and the many-colored coat, Noah and the ark he built, and many others. To this day I vividly remember these stories.

When I was in high school, I taught a Sunday school class. Today I am still very active in my church, holding any job that needs to be filled. Life is good. We have to accept it as it comes to us. Be happy with our family and friends. As friends move away or die, we must keep making new friends. At my age, life is drawing its curtain on me, but every day seems sweeter. Every flower gives more pleasure. Every bird singing as the sun comes up lifts my spirit for the day. I feel blessed.

Mrs. Bernice Ash with doll dressed for Goodfellows and one of her handmade quilts, Christmas 1997

Mrs. Helen Lemke

"When there is too much pressure, I just say a prayer. If that doesn't help, I just say another, and another."

I was born in 1915. The place was Yukon, Pennsylvania. It was a coal-mining town. My parents came from Poland. My father came first in 1900, and my mother, brother, and two sisters came six months later. None of them could speak English. My mother couldn't read or write. She never went to school. She had four daughters and seven sons. My parents gave us a lot of love. I don't ever remember being hungry. We were a happy family.

I didn't get much schooling. I wanted to be a schoolteacher so much. Fifth grade was all I got. I started to work at the age of nine and a half. I worked in a butcher shop and I didn't work full time. I got my working papers at the age of twelve. My mother didn't want her boys to work in the mines, so we all moved to Hamtramck, Michigan, the year of 1928. I got a job three days after we got there, working as a dishwasher in a restaurant. I got one dollar per day, twelve hours of work a day, and no days off. I had to work; the Depression hit. It was hard and I gave up school to help. My dad wouldn't take welfare. He was in his seventies and got a job as a nightguard. When the school census came to check the students, my mother felt bad. She told them I was a niece who was just visiting.

In 1933, I met my husband, a Detroit police officer. I was eighteen and he was twenty-eight. We were married for fifty-eight years when he died. Clyde retired as a police lieutenant. We had three sons and one daughter. The three boys went to the Vietnam War. I'm so grateful because they all came back home. My oldest was a lieutenant colonel in the Air Force.

Sometimes people ask me about my way of thinking. I feel like I'm the luckiest person in the world. My parents were very loving. My three sons came home from the war. I have a wonderful daughter. They married wonderful people, and I treat them like my own kids. They make my sons and daughter happy. There's nothing I wouldn't do for them. I'm very open. "If I can't say something nice. . ." I like to see people happy.

I had a wonderful husband whom I loved very much to the end. I know he felt the same way about me. I love people. I don't care if they are black or white. I just look at life differently. We all were blessed and put here on this earth. It is up to us to be good or bad. All the good Lord does is give us strength and courage whenever we need it. No matter how bad we think we feel, it could be worse.

When I meet another senior citizen, it seems like we say, "The Golden Years — where are they?" They're here! Just open your eyes and look around. If you give a little of yourself, you will get twice as much back. Try to help someone. Do your part. I promise it will come out twice as good. When there is too much pressure, I just say a prayer. If that doesn't help, I just say another, and another. You'd be surprised how much it helps. It takes the pressure off.

Mr. Richard Moore

"When his mother called and told me I am his hero, I was floored!"

To be considerate of family members and people you come in contact with throughout your lifetime is the basis of my philosophy. What a challenge!

As a father of five children — one son and four daughters — plus a grandfather of twenty grandchildren — ten boys and ten girls, the oldest sixteen and the youngest one year of age — I have to be aware of what I say, and know that the actions I take will be an example to all of them as they grow up.

It wasn't until I went into the service that I realized how much my father's philosophy and values influenced my life. I joined the Marine Corps during the Korean War — the most disciplined and strictest branch of the service at the time. During boot camp, I wrote my dad and thanked him for the example he had set for me as I grew up. The training got me through boot camp and also my years in the Corps. I try to set the same example for my kids — in work, with people, and with their own family members.

My work ethic has always been to give one hundred percent to my employer, regardless of the job. In the forty-two years I enjoyed with one employer and seven with another, I can honestly say I always did my very best. I have seen this same standard carried on by my own son, daughters, and my sons-in-law. Now I see my grandkids doing the same, whether it is in school, work, sports, or just household chores.

It's easy to quote the Golden Rule but to follow it is often difficult. I have tried to instill its meaning in my family by example, in regard to all people. There is no greater compliment, as far as I'm concerned, than to over-

Mr. Richard Moore, 1998

hear my kids or grandkids say, "Grandpa says," or "Grandpa would have done it this way." Just recently, one of my grandsons, age nine, had to do a school project. He had to build a monument and explain its meaning to his classmates. The monument was to be of his number one hero. When his mother called and told me I am his hero, I was floored!

To make mistakes and to admit them, and to help people without seeking payment or recognition are other examples I try to set. As the years go by, it's very gratifying to know that you've made a difference in the way so many lives have been shaped. Philosophy and values go pretty much hand in hand. I think I have unconsciously given mine to at least thirty people I know of, and hopefully a lot more.

Mrs. Martha Rockefeller

*"Be a good girl, be responsible, be kind, love, and
develop a good attitude."*

W hen I made my appearance in the world on August 21,
1918, it was in the home in which I would live for nine
years. It was also in this house, at age nine, that I talked
to my dying mother. The day before her death she took my hand and
said to me, "Be a good girl, be responsible, be kind, love, and develop
a good attitude."

I didn't understand these words, so my mother wrote them down
for me. They were like the word God. You can't feel or see them, but
you know they will help shape your life. She had underlined the words
responsible, love and good attitude.

During Thanksgiving 1926 my mother was preparing our traditional dinner of turkey, dressing, cranberry sauce, and pumpkin pie
when a neighbor lady stopped by. She was crying because she didn't
have food for her family of five. My mother packed up the meal she
had cooked, put it in our red wagon and took it to this woman's home.
For our dinner we had a two-quart jar of chicken, which my mother
had canned.

A similar incident was repeated twenty-eight years later when my daughter, Pat, came home and was crying because a very dear friend of hers wasn't having Thanksgiving because both parents weren't working. They had no electricity and no food. After a big discussion, we decided we would have our Thanksgiving later. My daughter went to the garage, got her red wagon down from where it was stored, and used it to take the meal to her friend's house.

Mrs. Martha Rockefeller, 1998

When I see a red wagon today, I picture Thanksgiving being taken to someone less fortunate. I have lived as my mother asked me to, and I can say that after all these years I know what those words mean. I still have them.

Part Four

To My Children

*Each year on my children's birthdays, I write a letter to them.
I share with Emily or Jason what I have learned in my life, so that it
will be of benefit to them, particularly someday when I am no longer here.*

—Thomas P. Waldinger

March 1998

Dear Emily,

There are qualities about you that are remarkable. Whenever we spend time together or talk, you make me feel better. That's a gift. I have also noticed that you share this attribute with family, your friends, and people you meet. This is important because it has a positive effect on those around you.

Other special qualities you have are the joy, laughter, sense of humor, and sparkle that you bring to each day. It's fun and exciting to be your father.

I admire your sensitivity and caring for family and friends. You always have a genuine interest in others. Your Grandpa Herman once told me that truly remarkable people do things for others when it is not convenient or when it may be difficult for them. You have shared that trait with me many times.

One of my greatest joys is seeing these remarkable qualities in you and knowing that you will accomplish great things in the future. Carl Sandburg wrote the following poem. It reflects my feelings about you:

"I love you for what you are
knowing so well what you are.
And I love you more yet, child,
deeper yet than ever, child,
for what you are going to be,
knowing so well you are going far,

knowing your great works are ahead,
ahead and beyond,
yonder and far over yet."

Happy Birthday.

Love,

Dad

Emily Waldinger, Leland, Michigan, 1989

Remember Our Love

To My Daughter, Emily

Come with me
On life's journey
My Emily
You and me
My Emily.

When I feel alone
I think of your smile
Hear your laughter
I know then
Why I am here
Life's meaning
Becomes clear
You and me
My Emily.

I fell in love
The moment you were born
You are special
The way you make me feel
A permanent peace
In a world of change.

There will be times in your life
When you doubt yourself
Feel alone and unsure
Remember our love
Remember your faith
Seek the truth

My soul is with you always
My soul is with you always.

When the morning light
Wakes you each day
Remember our love
Remember your faith
When I'm no longer
On this earth.

In the early spring
See the peonies in bloom
Place lilacs in your room
Permanent beauty
In a world of change
Remember our love
Remember your faith
When I'm no longer
On this earth.

I fell in love
The moment you were born
You are special
The way you make me feel
A permanent peace
In a world of change
My soul is with you always
My soul is with you always
I love you forever
I love you forever.

— Thomas P. Waldinger

Forever And Always

To My Daughter, Emily

Smiles and kisses
Eyes that sparkle
Hugs that caress my soul
Greetings at home
Never alone
The one who makes me whole.

Smiles and kisses
Blueberry buckle
Stars that paint the sky
Forever and always
In this world
My little girl.

The moment I see you
My heart soars
I am forever yours
Walks in the park
Talks after dark
My little girl.

You take me places
I've never been
The world opens its arms
Your hand in mine
We move in time
Forever my little girl.

The moment I see you
My heart soars
I am forever yours
Forever and always
In this world
My little girl.

— Thomas P. Waldinger

October 1996

Dear Jason,

The day you were born, I looked into your eyes and you had this great smile on your face. Everything that is wonderful and good in the world, I saw at that moment and continue to see in you every day. I admire your honesty and integrity.

In your life, you will have challenges to overcome. It is your response to these challenges that is important. Faith, love, humor, acceptance, forgiveness, and compassion are some of the tools God has given you to aid you in your time of need and in your response.

Mom and I will always be there for you as well. The following blessing, given to me by a friend, has great meaning to me:

"I pray that you will be
strong in trial,
wise in confusion,
calm in chaos, and
abounding in love.

May others look to you for
understanding when troubled,
hope when tested,
courage when frightened, and
a brother when alone.

May God bless all of your comings and goings,
May He bless every life you touch.

May He bless your accomplishments
and fulfill your dreams.
And, at the end of each day,
may you rest with the assurance
that you have been a
good and faithful servant.
May God bless you today and always."

Happy Birthday.

Love,

Dad

Jason Waldinger with father, Dr. Thomas Waldinger,
Ann Arbor, Michigan, 1988

Beyond Imagination

To My Son, Jason

Hello, my son
You've just been born
With you in my arms
A new life begins.

Beyond imagination
Wondrous celebration
With you in my arms
A new life begins.

Everything good
And wonderful
In this world
I see at this moment
Peaceful sensation
Beyond imagination
Wondrous celebration.

The first day of school
Mom watches her little boy
Tear on her cheek
Heart pounding
The world awaits
You are the one
My only son.

The light in your room
Calls me in the evening
Nighttime stories

Baseball glories
You are the one
My only son.

You be the ball
I'll be the glove
Your hand in mine
We move in time
Forever is my love
Like the heavens above.

I'm looking up at you now
Everything good and wonderful I see
Every day, every moment
Beyond imagination
Wondrous celebration
Peaceful sensation.

You be the ball
I'll be the glove
Your hand in mine
We move in time
Forever is my love
Like the heavens above.

— Thomas P. Waldinger

Crimson Clouds

To Emily and Jason

Walk alone in the woods, my child
Be at one with God
See the pillars of life
Appreciate the fragrance of creation
Be at one with God.

Walk alone on the beach, my child
Be at one with God
Listen to the rhythm of the waves
Feel the wind
Its strength and softness
Ever changing
Like life itself
Be at one with God.

Walk alone in the meadow, my child
Be at one with God
Sense the vastness
Of the universe
I love you
More than that
My sweet child
More than that.

Walk with me, my child
Our hands become one
The sun is setting
The clouds are crimson

Let me share
My prayer for you.

Let your soul be your guide
Let your heart be filled with joy
Let love dwell within
Let your thoughts
Be at one with God.

Always know
I am still here
Still here my sweet child
Through my love
Through my love.

— Thomas P. Waldinger

Part Five

Faith

Nothing in life is more wonderful than faith —
the one great moving force which we can neither
weigh in the balance nor test in the crucible.

— Sir William Osler

Mrs. Helen Holody

"For what does it profit a man . . ."

Looking back on my life from the vantage point of my fifty-seventh year reveals how loving was that counsel provided by our Lord when He wisely advised, "For what does it profit a man if he gain the whole world and suffer the loss of his soul." In retrospect, I see how this admonition has directly influenced how I live and the decisions I make. Life is a journey, and how I live this life will determine what kind of an afterlife I will have.

Many other influences have also contributed to my philosophy of life. My life has been blessed by Providence with wonderful parents, a loving and devoted husband, and good, faithful children. First, it was my parents who gave me their philosophy of life through their love, discipline, sacrifices, and example. I was the second oldest in a family of seven children. My parents always demonstrated much love for us, which included the right amount of discipline. Their sacrifices were numerous, one of the biggest of which was putting all of us through parochial school, which had a major impact on my life. Most important of all was their example. They not only taught us how to live but also showed us. They were extremely devoted to one another, always putting their Catholic faith and God first in their lives. Their marriage was a mirror of the Trinity — my father, my mother, and God. They were happy, not because there were no trials, but because they had the hope that faith in God and His promised afterlife ensures.

We had our share of tragedies. My youngest sister, Anita, was born with cerebral palsy along with a spastic condition, which left her like a baby all her life. She could not sit unassisted, let alone walk and talk and use her hands. My parents believed that God gave them this special soul to care for until He called her home. And so they cared for her (especially my mother) in their home until my mother became ill with cancer and Anita was put in a nursing home nearby. Every day, my mother went to the nursing home to feed my sister lunch and dinner but, more than that, to give her love and affection. When my mother died, my father took over this role, caring for Anita until her death at the age of thirty-three.

I remember when I was in college, someone had advised my parents that they should put my sister in a nursing home because her presence in our home might ruin their children's chances of finding a husband or wife. I told my mother, "I wouldn't have wanted to marry the kind of man who wouldn't want to marry me because of Anita."

Another tragedy that occurred at the beginning of my senior year in high school was the death of my brother, who was two years younger than I. He was accidentally shot in the back of the head while hunting with some acquaintances from school. The young man who shot him was devastated. He apologized to my parents and asked their forgiveness. My parents and all of us forgave him, but it was extremely difficult. Without God and our Catholic faith and the hope that it gave us, we could not have forgiven the young man nor made it through those difficult days after my brother's death. The impact of my brother's death on my life was far-reaching. I had heard it said over and over that I should live my life as if I would die tomorrow because I do not know when God will call me home. But somehow I didn't think it would ever happen to me. I pictured myself living to a ripe old age. Then suddenly my brother, who was very close to me, died at fifteen years of age. This was the cause of much reflection on my own life. I suddenly realized that the Lord could call me home at an early age and that I must be ready to meet Him.

At the recent canonization of Edith Stein, Pope John Paul II noted that suffering pointed the way to the truth of the cross when he said, "Don't accept anything as truth if it is without love. And don't accept anything as love if it is without truth. One without the other is a harmful lie. . . . Many of our contemporaries would want the cross made silent. The true message of pain is a lesson of love. Love makes pain bear fruit and pain deepens love."

From my perspective now, and considering his comments, I can see a deeper lesson about evil in these two events. The suffering by my sister, Anita, and the devotion with which first my mother and then my father cared for her showed how pain is compelling testimony of love to those, such as me, who are blessed to witness it in truth. Selfless love of life is victor over lifeless love of the self. In the death of my brother, one can see an especially unspeakable evil, the wanton and impersonal universe of the nihilist, where random acts show that if there is a God, He is reckless and uncaring, and therefore not to be relied upon. Here a simple and direct forgiveness of an inestimable grievance transforms an otherwise horrid universe into a poignant reminder of another great admonition of our Lord, "to be in the world, but not of the world." When I was in high school, a nun in one of my religion classes once said, "When you look for a husband or wife, you should choose someone who will help you get to heaven." And my grandmother told me that you do not reach heaven or hell alone; you always bring somebody with you. With this in mind, I married my loving and devoted husband of thirty-five years. Paul has been the greatest influence in my life. Certainly he has been one of God's greatest gifts to me. Possessing a keen mind and a quick wit, he has shown much wisdom throughout his life. My husband has been a source of great strength for me because he is a man of principle who has the courage of his convictions. He is not afraid to say no when everyone else is saying yes.

We have grown in our faith together, often struggling to make sense of all the changes occurring in the Catholic Church after Vatican

II. Our biggest struggle has been in raising our three sons with traditional values when the world surrounding us has been just the opposite. When our boys were ready for school, we sent them to a newly founded, parent-run Catholic school. This was not an easy choice, because many hours were spent volunteering on various committees for fundraising, teacher selection, and so on. I served on its board for eight years, four years as president. However, long-lasting friendships were formed with other parents sending their children to this special school. Their influence provided us with the strength and the courage necessary to make hard decisions in our faith and in the raising of our children. It seems our efforts have been rewarded because our sons, who are now in their late twenties and early thirties, share our traditional values and are strong in their faith.

As my husband and I approach our sixties and our sons are getting married, we look forward to grandchildren, retirement, and whatever else Providence has for us, and — should we be so presumptuous — to what St. Augustine spoke of when he said, "Our hearts shall not rest until they rest in Thee."

Mrs. Helen Holody and family, Salzburg, Austria, August 1988

Mrs. Dorothy Mundle

"I am still learning and seeking."

I have been surrounded by good people all my life — my parents, my two sisters, my husband, and my children. I was born in Carleton, Michigan, in 1919. After high school, I graduated from business college. I married when I was twenty-one. Ron and I had three children, two of whom preceded us in death — Linda and Roland Jr. Valerie is a blessing in our life. I have two beloved grandchildren, Anna and Joe. My dear husband died in 1996, after a long battle with Parkinson's disease. I am alone now for the first time in my life. I am living in an apartment in a retirement village. Life is like a roller-coaster ride, with many ups and downs.

I remember two turning points in my life. First, when I was in my mid-thirties, while sweeping the kitchen floor, I thought, "I sweep this floor today and tomorrow I must sweep it again. Is this what life is about?" Then, in my sixties while attending a Bible class, the teacher mentioned John 5:24: "I tell you the truth, whoever hears my words and believes Him who sent me has eternal life, and will not be condemned; he has crossed over from death to life." I realized I did not need to die to have eternal life. It was mine now. What a comfort.

I am still learning and seeking. However, some thoughts have sustained me over the years. I am God's child and everyone I meet is a child of God. I need to have a church family. I try to live by the Golden Rule. I try to be optimistic and look on the bright side. Money and books are just paper if not shared. Before I can help someone, I must have my own house in order. As I grow older, I find myself seeking to accept, rather than to understand. I am grateful for the privilege of a lifetime on God's beautiful planet.

Ron and Dot Mundle, 1989

Anonymous Patient

"He said to me that the more you give to charities, churches, or temples, the more you get in return. You must leave the world a better place when you die."

This is about my husband. He was raised by parents who left Germany because of the conditions in that country before World War II. They were aware of trouble happening in their country. Their goal was to either come to the U.S. or go to South America. Because an aunt was already here and loved America, they decided to join her. His parents always had refugees from Europe living in their home. My husband's family consisted of two parents, four brothers, one sister, and himself. He was the youngest. They always had four to six other people sharing their home, food and clothing. The families would stay about a year, get a job, save some money, and then move on. Meanwhile, another family would arrive. They had only four bedrooms. Each set of parents had a bedroom and the other two bedrooms were assigned one for the girls and the other for the boys.

Through junior high school, my husband shared a twin bed with his brother. One slept at the top and the other at the bottom of the bed. Finally, in high school, he had his own twin bed. His brothers all joined the Army when they were through with school. World War II was in progress. He thought nothing of it. Sharing was something he was brought up to do. Also, his parents wanted the children to speak English and insisted on speaking it in the home. They were in the United States now and it was important to speak English and not German.

When my husband joined the Army after high school, he was excited to be able to travel and serve his country. Also, living with many people together in a barracks made him feel right at home. Many of the other soldiers complained about sleeping in a big room with many other soldiers, so my husband would tell them he was used to it. They had their own bed and they shouldn't complain.

He was chosen to be in the Army band and went to Japan in 1948. In 1950, the Korean War broke out and he was one of the first solders to arrive in the beginning of July to fight the North Koreans. He was thirty-five miles from the Yule River in China when, on Thanksgiving Day, the Chinese Communists became involved and the soldiers had to retreat to the thirty-eighth parallel. He was lucky to survive. Many of his friends were captured and killed. When it was time for him to come home after serving his one year, President Truman made an order extending everyone's time in the service for another year, so he was forced to stay in Korea. He made it home with many honors including the Bronze Star. He was very patriotic. Our big U.S. flag was always flown on holidays. About twenty soldiers he served with in Korea remained friends and we often had reunions. "A person becomes very close to people who lived in foxholes together," he would always say to me.

Upon his discharge from the Army, he came home and started college. That's where I met him, in an English class on Shakespeare. We fell in love. Neither set of parents was happy about us marrying each other. He was Jewish and I was Christian. This was a major problem for everyone except us. Forty-two years ago this was very unusual. We decided to celebrate all holidays with each family so no one would be hurt.

We had four children — two boys and two girls. Only the girls survived. He taught our girls that they were put on earth to benefit society and to make the world a better place in which to live. He always felt a parent should give his children confidence in themselves. He taught them when they were little that they must go to college and do their best in whatever they chose to do. Both of our girls are engineers. Both are doing very well.

My husband wrote short stories, poetry, and children's stories. He oil-painted, did watercolor, wrote music and lyrics. He played many instruments including the saxophone, clarinet, flute, organ, piano and guitar. He was very artistic and talented. Moreover, my husband requested nothing for himself —no gifts — but always gave in return. He gave flowers, cards, poetry, gifts, and money to students and paid for dinners anonymously.

He was a member of the Masonic organization and worked with the youth groups in the state of Michigan. When someone needed money for tuition or books, he would always help. There were many times I would have money saved for something like a dishwasher or a microwave and it would disappear because some student needed help and the money was used for that person. He said to me that the more you give to charities, churches, or temples, the more you get in return. You must leave the world a better place when you die.

I was very ill many times during our marriage. I lost two babies, had blood clots and many surgeries, but he was always at my side, encouraging me to get well. I became injured at work and he retired to be at home to help me. He made me get out of bed, get dressed every day, and get moving. He took me to lunch, to shop, or just to walk around the block. Without his encouragement, I would not have made it.

In the summer of 1996, he started having trouble with his stomach. He had a yearly physical so he thought it was something minor, but it was cancer of the colon. The cancer had spread to his lymph nodes, liver, and kidney. The doctors gave him only six weeks to six months to live. He ended up living a year and a half. He was on chemotherapy most of the time. He knew he was dying. There were many discussions on what to do after he was gone, such as what people and charities to give money to. He would tell me that you have achieved success when you love, laugh, and live well, and leave children on earth to carry on.

He wrote a Christmas carol and gave it to my church in my honor. The church dedicated the song to him and sang it in church four days before he died. He heard it on a tape they made for him. It made him very happy. The song is beautiful. Both a Christian minister and a rabbi visited him in the hospital. They both prayed with him. His wish was to die at home, but that is not what happened. The whole month of December 1997 he was in the hospital dying. I was there every day to try to encourage him to get better so he could come home. He wanted to have potato pancakes on Hanukkah, but instead they had a respirator doing his breathing for him. He became better and the doctors took the respirator off on Tuesday afternoon — the beginning of Hanukkah. He said he would never have the respirator on him again.

The following day his breathing was more labored and the doctors wanted him to be put on the respirator again. He said no more life support machinery. He said he had enough and was ready to die. I stayed with him till the end, talking to him, holding his hand, petting him, and telling him how much I loved him.

When my husband died, I kissed him goodbye, pulled away from him, and at the same time a white smoke or white cloud left his head and body. The top of his bed was facing some dark windows so it was very noticeable. I thought I was seeing something that wasn't there, but the male nurse attending him also saw it. This had to be his spirit leaving him to go to heaven. He died about six o'clock on Christmas morning, Jesus's birthday. He made it through his holiday and died on my holiday. I really felt comfort knowing he was in heaven with God.

Because he died during the holidays, we thought many people would not be at the funeral home. To my surprise, hundreds of people came and paid their respects to him and me. I have since received many letters from young people, telling me how he had helped them either with advice, a few words of encouragement, or money. The doctors who assisted him wrote letters telling me how much they admired him and would always remember him. After living with such a great man, I could never marry again. I do not want anything but to be with him forever when I die.

※

Mr. Milo Teer

*"I make other transplant patients realize
that they are not alone."*

I started as a patient with Dr. Ulrich in 1970. I was always impressed with the manner in which he treated all his patients. He was never in a hurry and always took time to talk to you. Every office visit would start with "How are you?" to my wife, our son, and me. At each subsequent visit, Dr. Ulrich always remembered what I had told him about my family's activities on my previous visit. In all of our talks he never failed to say, "Praise God" or "Thank God," and he would always end our visit with, "God bless you."

I remember when Dr. Ulrich told me he was getting ready to retire and was looking for a replacement. I was confident he would leave his patients in good hands. I met Dr. Waldinger during an appointment in 1985. I still remember coming home and telling my wife that Dr. Ulrich had found a doctor just like him to take over his dermatological practice.

All was good in my life — a good marriage, a nice son, a great job, and good health. As time passed, however, I found I couldn't finish my daily three-mile run, an activity I enjoyed every morning. In just a little over a week's time I saw my internist, who said I should consult a

Mr. Milo Teer, Transplant Olympics,
400 yard dash, 1998

heart specialist. The heart doctor told me that my heart was double its normal size as a result of a heart disease called cardiomyopathy. I was sent home with little hope and told to get my things in order. This took place in the summer of 1981. The doctor's advice was very close to the truth.

During the next two years, my health deteriorated quickly. I was admitted into the hospital for congestive heart failure on several occasions. At the beginning of 1984, I grew steadily worse. Two heart specialists at the University of Michigan Hospital told my wife and me that my only hope was a heart transplant. A call was received on April 30, 1984, that a heart had been located for me. On May 1, 1984, I received my heart transplant.

Many friends have asked how I was able to cope with the turn of events in my life. I had been in and out of the hospital for two years, received a heart transplant, and yet was uncertain about what the future had in store for me. I can, however, think of many reasons why I am a survivor. The primary reason was my faith in God and completely trusting in Him. My faith carried me through the first thirty-eight years of my life and why shouldn't it carry me through my remaining years? I really believe that He will not bestow upon me more than I am able to handle. We are never to question what He sends our way. Before and during all my medical procedures, I say my prayers. I pray that He will give me the strength to accept His will. When I pray, I always include a prayer for my doctors. I ask that God will guide their hands and bless them for their dedication to their patients. Along with my faith in God is my complete trust in my doctors.

I've encountered other medical problems since my heart transplant, mainly skin cancer and a serious vascular disease which affects my legs. I am very lucky that my doctors are so dedicated in treating my physical problems, but also are truly concerned with the quality of my life. I try not to dwell on my problems but rather focus on all the good things in my life. I hope that I'm a good role model, especially to transplant recipients. I make other transplant patients realize they are not alone.

Mrs. Betty Smith

"Doing God's work on earth."

I have been aware of the actions of many people in my life, but the one who made the greatest impression was Jesse, my best friend — my husband of forty-seven years.

He was a quiet man with a slight speech impediment, which did not prevent him from showing compassion for his fellow man. This was evident in the hours he spent helping hospitalized veterans, neighbors, and family.

Because of him I have become a more thoughtful and caring person by doing for others. My philosophy is, "Doing God's work on earth."

Two weeks before my husband's death I found the following prayer in my Bible. I know it tells what a "friend" I had.

I Said a Prayer for You Today

I said a prayer for you today and know God
must have heard. I felt the answer in my heart
although He spoke no word.

I didn't ask for wealth or fame. I knew you
wouldn't mind.

I asked Him to send treasures of a far more
lasting kind. I asked that He'd be near you
at the start of each new day.

To grant you health and blessings and friends
to share your way. I asked for happiness for
you in all things great and small, but it was for
His loving care I prayed for most of all.

This prayer was read at his funeral by our minister. Six months
after Jesse's death, I returned to school and graduated in 1996 with a
degree in gerontology at the age of seventy-one. At the present time, I
do volunteer work at the Veterans Hospital in Allen Park one morning
a week. On Wednesdays I am a facilitator for a senior citizen grief support group that meets in Dearborn Heights.

I am grateful that I can continue to serve God and my fellow man.

Betty and Jesse Smith attend Harvest Dinner
at church, 1993

Mrs. Bernice Lezotte

"Bear ye one another's burdens."

I was born in Windsor, Ontario, Canada, and came to the Downriver area with my parents and older sister when I was two years old. A brother was later born here. None of my grandparents, aunts, uncles, or cousins chose to follow us to the United States so we were raised without an extended family. All of my relatives are still in Canada or England. Being without family here, we made the church the center of our life for spiritual and social activities. As a young girl I belonged to a church group whose motto was, "Bear ye one another's burdens," and that became my philosophy and aim in life.

I have been a caregiver most of my married life. My mother-in-law became a widow at the age of sixty-six and simply gave up any interest in life. My husband and I cared for all her needs until she died at the age of eighty-nine. Our middle son has Down syndrome. For the first eight years of his life, it was a struggle to keep him alive. During the past several years, he has suffered from a severe heart problem and it is difficult to make him comfortable. His pediatrician when he was young allowed us to visit many parents of newborn Down syndrome children. We attempted to give them some insight into the problems and joys they would encounter in their child's life. It was a very rewarding experience. Throughout my son's life, we have been and continue to be active in the local and state Association for Retarded Citizens. These organizations brought us together with many caring and concerned parents trying to do their best for their children. Moreover, school and church afforded more caregiving activities to me. For the past two years, since my husband's death, I have been volunteering for the hospice group that cared for him in his final days.

Music has also been a special gift in my life. I was awarded a high school letter for solo work. I still sing at weddings and funerals and am a member of my church choir. My mother and father sang in choirs, and my father-in-law had a magnificent voice and sang for forty years in his church. My husband was blessed with both an exceptional speaking and singing voice and sang in his church choir as well as producing a minstrel show in the early 1950s. Although my husband and I were of different faiths and attended different churches, we always helped one another with various musical events as needed. Our youngest son enjoys playing the guitar and our oldest son, an attorney, has joined with several other attorney friends to produce musicals. They have performed all over the state of Michigan and elsewhere. I like to think that over the years we have been able to give many others pleasurable moments of inspiration and fun.

I have some treasured memories of the day my husband died. Although he had heart problems for twenty-three years, he died of cancer in four short months. The last five days, my husband was under hospice care. The last two days, they moved a hospital bed into our bedroom next to the double bed we had shared for the past forty-eight and a half years. It was Super Bowl Sunday and our oldest grandson would come in and out of the bedroom, reporting the scores to his grandpa. At one point, our grandson and granddaughter, five and two years old at the time, were bouncing up and down on our double bed, and my little grandson, in a singsong voice, said, "Grandma is taking care of Grandpa and we're keeping him company." And keep him company we did. The whole family was there until the moment of his death.

Looking back on all of this, I am reminded of the last line of the Prayer of the Anonymous Confederate Soldier which reads, "I am among all men most richly blessed."

Mrs. Marianne Glinn

"Our captain received two SOS calls from ships, but it was too late to save them."

Seeing the movie *Titanic* recently stirred up a lot of horrific memories for me. In 1929, when I was six years old, my parents came from Germany on a ship called *Bremen*, which was claimed to be the largest steamship in the world.

We left Bremerhaven in December, the first Sunday in Advent, and ran into the worst storm in forty years — a hurricane. Our captain disobeyed orders to return, claiming he could make the trip in three days. It took thirteen. I found out since that many prayers were said for our small family, both in that small village in Germany and also in the U.S.

The papers were filled with articles about the ship in distress. Our captain received two SOS calls from ships, but it was too late to save them. Our cabin filled with water to the point that we had to move in with another family.

This experience so affected my life that to this day I will not go on a ship where I cannot see both shores. I also have often wondered why the Lord spared us and for what purpose. It truly strengthened my faith in Him. Also, why were we spared the terrible times people went

Mrs. Marianne Glinn, 1930

through in Germany during World War II? That question was made clear to me recently after a visit from a German cousin.

I had very God-fearing parents for whom I am deeply grateful, and I always tried to instill that faith in my children and grandchildren. It seems that whatever trials and tribulations life deals us, the Lord is there with us and we are never alone.

Although my parents are both gone now, I'll never forget what a great influence they had on my life and how much help they were to me and my family when my marriage broke up. Also, Dr. Ulrich was a wonderful help and confidant during those trying times. I will never forget him and how he helped me make many wise decisions, particularly concerning my youngest son, whom I had to raise alone. I often think the rare affliction I had at that time was for a purpose. Otherwise, I never would have met Dr. Ulrich. The Lord works in mysterious ways.

Mr. Charles Hambel

"This man is caring, so put him in the Medical Corps."

My road to life started by coming from a very poor family of eleven children. I was the second eldest. Growing up back then was very difficult with little money and material things. We managed to do okay. No one, however, told me I was going to be the caregiver for my mother.

Our home had no bath or running water, so I did all the carrying of water to our home. I did this for many years until we were able to move to better surroundings. I graduated from high school, but was unable to go to college. I secured several jobs until I was finally drafted into the U.S. Army and experienced all the "goodies" of basic training. It seems God said to the Army, "This man is caring, so put him in the Medical Corps." They did, and I served in Korea for two years, tending to the wounded.

After my career in the service for two years, I returned home safe and sound and resided in Ohio for about four years. I then relocated to Michigan, married, and started my banking career. I received assistance from a friend of my wife's family. I could see and really watched how this friend loved and cared for his customers. This was "right up

Mr. Charles Hambel in Japan,
en route to Korea, 1951

my alley" because I loved to help everyone. I continue to always go out of my way to help others.

The following story now comes to mind. When I became a bank branch manager several years later, a customer came to the door of the bank before we were open in the morning. I went to the door and asked him what he wanted and he said he needed to get a haircut. He seemed very sad. I said to him, "Let me give you the money." He returned later and was so happy. To this day, I still love to be of help to anyone in need. I know God had plans thirteen years ago as He put His loving hands on me and I survived a bout with cancer.

Mrs. Isabelle McCarthy

*"Do everything you can to solve your problem
and then turn the problem over to God."*

I came from a family of four — a mother, a father, and an older sister. I was raised in a Christian atmosphere both at home and in school. Through the years I have had a good marriage, eight children, and twenty-two grandchildren. Moreover, I've developed a strong faith in God, and have tried to be a follower of His Ten Commandments.

One thing I have found to be very successful in my life: "Ask and you shall receive." When troubled and in doubt, my mind flustered, I ask God to help me make the right decision. Sometimes waiting for discernment requires patience. However, when the time comes that a decision or necessary action must be taken, I find I have reached a determination, found an answer to the problem, and it's always satisfying in the sense that I feel peaceful about it. The philosophy here may be, "Do everything you can to solve your problem and then turn the problem over to God." It works for me and is very comforting.

My feelings regarding death are that even though my husband is now deceased after forty-eight years of marriage and I live alone, I will always enjoy the company of our Lord. What makes the death of a loved one or the thought of one's own death bearable is the belief in eternal life. The following is a prayer that I try to say daily. It seems to encompass so much that it can possibly be considered the embodiment of Christian principles.

Lord, Make Me an Instrument of Thy Peace

Where there is hatred, let me sow love;
Where there is injury, pardon;
Where there is doubt, faith;
Where there is darkness, light;
And where there is sadness, joy.

O Divine Master, grant that I may not
so much seek to be consoled as to console;
To be understood as to understand;
To be loved, as to love;
For it is in giving that we receive;
It is in pardoning that we are pardoned;
And it is in dying that we are born to eternal life.

— Saint Francis of Assisi

Robert and Isabelle McCarthy, fiftieth high school class reunion, 1995

Mr. & Mrs. Walter Swanson

*Trust in the Lord with all your heart and lean not on
your own understanding; in all your ways acknowledge Him
and He will make your paths straight.*

— Proverbs 3:5 & 6 NIV

Our philosophy of how we approach life was formed in our childhood through our parents' belief in one God, the creator of the universe, revealed in the Bible as the source of all truth for living. Through experiences growing up, we had opportunities to examine this point of view for ourselves and concluded it was the right path to take.

When we met in our early twenties, our faith was the foundation for our individual lives and subsequently our married life together. It has guided us through fifty years of marriage and parenting, and we have never regretted our commitment to our biblical faith. When problems inevitably arose, we had in common the source of wisdom to find our way through them.

We also believe in remembering to be grateful for blessings in life. We are particularly thankful for our children and grandchildren and the joy and love they bring. We also developed many strong friendships through the years. Our friends have been with us through good times and bad and their concern, prayers, and genuine care have been invaluable additions to our lives.

Three passages in the Bible have been especially meaningful in guiding our path through life. They have provided us with direction, wisdom, and a sense of purpose throughout the years. Two verses come from the Old Testament and the third verse is found in the New Testament.

Marjorie and Walter Swanson, California, 1997

Trust in the Lord with all your heart and lean not on your own understanding; in all your ways acknowledge Him and He will make your paths straight.

— Proverbs 3:5 & 6 NIV

Remember your Creator in the days of your youth, before the days of trouble come and the years approach when you will say, "I find no pleasure in them."

— Ecclesiastes 12:1 NIV

We know that in everything God works for good, with those who love Him, who are called according to His purpose.

— Romans 8:28 RSV

Mrs. Marie Licari

"She said to me, 'Marie, live your life to the fullest.'"

T here are many philosophies that I live by but this one is by far the most important to me. My philosophy is to live life to the fullest.

In 1964, I was faced with a divorce and received custody of my five children. At that time, women's wages were not what they are today. Therefore, my children and I struggled greatly.

In my Golden Years, with sixteen grandchildren and five great-grandchildren so far, I am hopefully wiser. Life experiences of being a single parent and raising children alone taught me to always put God first. He has much to do with survival. Live your life to the fullest each day.

When I moved to Taylor, Michigan, I felt very low and depressed. I usually went to church every Sunday. After my move, I became involved with a church. There was a nun at the church who understood my feelings and got me involved in working at a nursing home as part of the Christian Service Commission. She said to me, "Marie, live your life to the fullest." I now do this, and as a result have become more religious. This has developed a deeper love for God. This particular person helped to form my philosophy of life. We still often have lunch together.

Mrs. Marie Licari (left) with Sister Jean Horger, 1999

Mr. Robert Fink

"All things come from God."

I was the only child of a beautiful young woman from Kentucky and a high-strung father from Illinois. Born in southwest Detroit in 1929, I had the wonderful experience of growing up with Grandma, Grandpa, two aunts, two uncles, Mom and Dad in a two-story, one-bath house. My mom and dad and I lived upstairs and Grandma and Grandpa downstairs. I lived downstairs most of the time. The neighborhood was a diverse melding of nationalities.

Growing up, I really enjoyed watching my grandma make bread and cook. In the late summer, trips to a farm market were the beginning of the canning season. All kinds of fruits and vegetables were canned. Everyone was involved. One of the things I still do to this day is chop my own cabbage for sauerkraut. I would also help braid rag rugs and played under the quilting frame (made by my dad) as my grandma and mother quilted.

My grandma's small bedroom off the kitchen was a place of pure ecstasy. Her bed was a homemade feather bed. What a joy it was to jump on the bed and sleep with Grandma. I started going to church with her at an early age. She would read stories to me from the Bible and quote scriptures from it on many subjects. She made sure I learned one verse a week for Sunday school. As I sit here today and think about her, I realize what a profound impact she had on my outlook on life: "All things come from God."

I am happy to be able to tell my grandchildren stories of the summers I spent on my great-aunt's farm in Illinois as a young boy — the nights with kerosene lamps, hand-cranked telephones, gasoline washing machines, drawing water from a cistern, slopping the hogs, gathering the eggs in the hen house, and catching a chicken for dinner for my aunt. She would wring its neck, feather and clean it. Years later, my wife witnessed such an event and could not eat the chicken for dinner. My Aunt Tess, with whom I stayed those summers, was my grandma's sister and she was also a very religious woman. Her many prayers and blessings will always be remembered by me.

I must tell you of an experience that revealed to me the power of having a strong faith in the healing power of the Lord Jesus Christ. As a young man, I had Meniere's disease, a condition which affects the inner ear. This lasted about five years. It left me totally immobile for as long as forty-eight hours or more at times. My Aunt Tess came to Michigan to visit that summer. No sooner had she seen me sick in bed, she was on her knees praying with a hand on my head. Through my faith and Jesus's healing power, my dizziness has not returned. "Wait on the Lord."

What a beautiful family I am blessed with now. My wife, Phyllis (we met in high school), and I have three wonderful sons. We waited eleven years for our first grandchild. A lovely lady reminded me to be patient. We are now blessed with seven beautiful grandchildren — three boys and four girls. When my three sons were growing up, I wanted them to learn to play a musical instrument, but they had no desire. I had studied music for many years, playing in schools, churches, weddings, and concerts. Now, years later, I'm able to hear my grandsons play the clarinet, French horn, and trumpet in concerts and see my granddaughters in their dance recitals.

The past forty-nine years have been with a person of unending love. Phyllis has always been there for me, especially the last seven months during my chemotherapy. Our life together has been, and will continue to be, a time of great joy and love, and the giving of our friendship to others.

Mr. Robert Fink, Chicago World's Fair, 1933

Mr. Ray Wolfe

"For God, all things are possible."

As a lay chaplain, I have had a number of unusual experiences that illustrate that with God all things are possible.

I was visiting with a young man who had been shot in the head while attending a social event. He was not the target of the shooter. Steve had a grazing wound and was getting well.

In the course of several visits, I met his mother and grandmother, who informed me that he was attending college and had good spiritual values and support. We prayed that God would heal him soon and he could complete his education.

Several weeks after his discharge, he was back in the hospital, much to my surprise. "Steve," I said, "How are you doing?" He replied, "I'm not sure. I have had blinding headaches for over a week. The doctors have examined me thoroughly and can't find any physical cause." "Well," I said, "Just the thought of being shot in the side of the head would give me a headache. It's a traumatic experience. Your denomination is Catholic and your parents tell me you have strong spiritual values. Do you believe you can be healed through prayer?"

Without hesitation, Steve said, "Yes, I do." As he sat on the edge of his bed, I stood before him and explained, "Steve, there are no guarantees. Nothing may happen, you may get well today, or it may take weeks or months."

As he sat on the bed, I stood in front of him and for some reason placed my hands with my palms over his eyes and fingers covering his temples. I said a brief extemporaneous prayer and removed my hands from him, really not knowing what to expect. "You won't believe this," Steve said, "My headache is gone." We thanked God in joint prayer and I left.

The lesson I learned from this was, "Don't sell prayer short." Matthew 19:26 says, "For God, all things are possible." You see, I wasn't expecting such immediate results. God has His own way of doing things.

Mr. Ray Wolfe, Grand Teton National Park, Wyoming, 1990

Mr. Carl Bissinger

"I was young at the time, but this experience and several others less threatening brought me to the realization that life is indeed fragile."

It was early in the morning on a cloudy but warm fall day. The year was 1944; the place somewhere in central Germany. Our infantry platoon was ordered to dig-in about two hundred yards from a farmhouse reported to be a German command post. We were deployed along a hedgerow, along a pile of firewood, and in a dilapidated shed used to house cattle. I was fortunate to be assigned a spot in the shed, which seemed at the time to offer the most protection from enemy gunfire.

I finished digging my ground cover, put my backpack just outside, and crawled in to rest before our hot meal would be served. Within a matter of minutes, we came under a severe mortar attack. There was no place to run or hide, so our only alternative was to hug the ground and pray. A shell landed within three feet of my position and a subsequent concussion literally lifted me about a foot from my foxhole. When the shelling stopped, I reached for my backpack to check for damage. There was nothing left but a small piece of burning canvas. I was young at the time, but this experience and several others less threatening brought me to the realization that life is indeed fragile.

When the war ended, I returned home to renew a friendship with a lovely young lady who had served four years as a nurse's aide at a veterans' hospital. She too had seen the high price many of our military had paid for our victory. When we married, we shared a similar appreciation of how true happiness can be found in the many things the Creator has provided — the flowers, the trees, the rain, and all the animals, large and small.

Mr. Carl Bissinger, 78th Infantry Division, Berlin, 1945

Mr. Joe Lee Robbins

But may it never be that I should boast except in the cross
of Lord Jesus Christ, by which the world has been crucified to me
and I to the world.

— Galatians 6:14

My high school American history teacher greatly admired Abraham Lincoln, who once said, "All that I am or ever hope to be, I owe to my darling mother." That caused me to begin to reflect on how much I owed to my wonderful mother, to whom I was so close. This closeness continued through high school, college, World War II, my marriage, and the rest of her life.

Our letters to each other were always very tender and touching. We cherished every opportunity we could get to talk to each other. Each one was always too short. She dearly, dearly loved my daddy and all of us children. I was the oldest of six, three boys and three girls.

When I was six years old, my four-year-old brother Billy and I stood on the bank of a mountain stream and watched as our mother and daddy were baptized into the membership of the Primitive Baptist Church in 1929. After that, we were taken to church regularly. My mother was never happier than when some of the church folks, especially the preachers, would come home with us and eat and stay all night. She delighted in talking endlessly with them about the Bible and the life of the church and its doctrine. Even after the company left, she would have Daddy sit down and tell her everything that he had talked about with them when she had to be out of earshot back in the kitchen, preparing the meals.

Mother, along with Daddy, greatly encouraged us in our school-work. As a result, all of us except one became college graduates.

They counseled us regularly on what good behavior meant and insisted that we "be good." She would say, "Now, Joe Lee, you are the oldest. The others will look up to you and I want you to set a good example for them. You know what certain other boys are doing that we don't like. We don't want you doing any of those things." You can imagine the positive reinforcement that was applied when necessary to ensure that these teachings were followed!

Daddy was a coal miner in Harlan County, Kentucky. He made a good living for us, and we never ran out of food, even in the Depression. Mother was very resourceful in preparing very nutritious and inexpensive meals. I still love her staples: bean soup, corn bread, fried potatoes, biscuits, oatmeal, flour gravy, fried bacon and, of course, all of the fruits and vegetables from the garden in their season.

She did all of this in houses with no running water, no refrigerator and no inside toilet. We lived in a very old farmhouse with no electricity on a two hundred-acre farm from 1938 to 1944, and water was drawn from a dug well. Largely due to her efforts, these were among the happiest years of our lives. I still remember the hymns I learned from listening to her sing as she did her work around the house and in the garden.

We identified with General Eisenhower, who said that his family was poor but didn't know it when he grew up on a farm in Kansas. Our parents were always able to give us something for Christmas. We played with some kids who didn't get anything.

I wanted to play on the football team in high school, but Daddy wouldn't let me. He let me play basketball. One day, when Daddy and I were watching Mother milk our cow, I asked him again to let me play football. He didn't say anything for a while, and then he said, "Joe Lee, do you see what a fine milk cow Old Jerz is?" I replied, "Of course I do. She gives us six gallons of milk a day and is as pretty as she can be!"

Mr. Joe Lee Robbins, Aviation Cadet, Army Air Force, San Antonio, Texas, 1945

He continued, "Do you think I would let her get all banged up and bruised playing football?" "No, sir!" I acknowledged. He explained, "Well, you know that I love you a whole lot more than I do this cow!" This story further represents the kind of wisdom that surrounded me while I was raised by this godly father and mother in the hills of Kentucky.

Daddy went to heaven in 1967 and Mother in 1973. I still feel a wonderful warmth in my heart as I reminisce about them and the good hugs that we exchanged every time we were together.

I graduated from the University of Kentucky in 1947 with a Bachelor of Science Degree in Metallurgical Engineering. I worked for three years as a metallurgist for Revere Copper and Brass in Detroit, then five years as general foreman of the rolling mill. I then worked for thirty years for Ford as a project engineer and was part of the management team of Ford Motor Company's Rouge Steel Mill in Dearborn, Michigan.

I have also been blessed by the godly influences of both my first and second wives, with whom I have three children and two stepchildren. We have been active in the Lord's work as Sunday school teachers, singers, youth workers, deacons, and I as an elder. I also helped organize the Downriver Detroit Christian Businessmen's Committee in 1967. This group held regular luncheon and dinner meetings where men told how they had accepted Jesus as their Savior and Lord, and then invited the guests to accept Him also.

After looking for many years for a Bible verse that seemed to explain "why I am who I am," I selected Galatians 6:14: "But may it never be that I should boast except in the cross of Lord Jesus Christ, by which the world has been crucified to me and I to the world."

Mrs. June Witthoff

*"I feel each hard time and sad time helped me
to be a stronger person."*

I was born in Sandwich (now Windsor), Ontario, Canada, on June 5, 1917. I am the firstborn of five children. My mother was a lovely, gentle woman and my father was a very intelligent, rather stern but kind man.

I grew up in the best of times. As children we were free to run and play, without the restriction of fear, all through our neighborhood with other children who came from similar families. The friends I had during those years are still friends to this day.

The Great Depression was a factor in our growing up. We had very little money, which didn't bother us as children. Of course, our friends also had very little money. We were all in the same circumstances and enjoyed simple and inexpensive pleasures together. This time in my life impressed on me the value of family, relationships, and people. We were not able to focus on material things for happiness. I learned our true needs were really few but always met. There was not any money for higher education after high school. It was hard to find employment, but luckily a friend of my dad's found a place for me to work in his business, so I went to work at eighteen and worked until I met and married my first husband, the father of my two very special sons. My husband died at a very young age and didn't live long enough to see how well his sons turned out. I am very proud of them and their wonderful families. I have grandchildren whom I love dearly.

After eleven years of widowhood, I married my present husband, Will, a fine and gentle man. We have been very fortunate to have traveled extensively in this country as well as Canada, the British Isles, Europe, and Asia.

Mrs. June Witthoff,
high school graduation, 1934

I am now living quietly with my husband of twenty-one years. We have a closeness with my sister and her husband, many dinners and excursions together, many family gatherings with nieces and nephews, and visits with my children and their families.

I have had a very good life with many ups and downs, good times and hard times. I feel each hard time and sad time helped me to be a stronger person. I have a strong faith in God and I believe in the power of love.

Mrs. Olive Sherby

"It has been said that life is a like a road well traveled with many risks. Many have traveled it before me and many will travel it after me. Those who have taken that road leave many lasting lessons we can glean from."

I was born May Olive Love in 1921, the middle child of five, all born in Canada. When I was five years old, my parents, like many from other countries, saw there were many more opportunities in the United States and so became U. S. citizens.

My childhood was a very happy one. I enjoyed school very much. The "Five Little Loves" grew close. My siblings were and are still very special to me. June, the first born in 1917, was beautiful and tall. We always looked to her as the big sister.

I remember, as a schoolgirl going to high school, that I always loved June's beautiful blue sweater. Because she went to school earlier than I did, I borrowed that sweater one day and returned it before she got home, carefully folding and returning it to her dresser. But somehow she knew. I guess I looked guilty.

My brother John (1919-1985) came next. He was a very handsome young man and very popular with the girls. He became an Eagle Scout. I remember my mother pinning his badge on his uniform at a special ceremony. He was an outstanding trumpet player and received a scholarship to Wayne State University to play in the university band.

He also served in the Army in Okinawa during World War II. A sudden heart attack took his life in 1985.

I was the entertainer in our family. I tap-danced, sang in the high school chorus and trio, sang with the dance band at school dances, and had the lead in the senior play. I was recognized at graduation as having never been absent or tardy through my entire twelve years of school.

Mrs. Olive Sherby, 1945

In 1924, brother Robert was born. He became a very popular dentist, practicing for forty years, and served in Korea in a M.A.S.H. unit as a dentist. He married his high school sweetheart.

Irene (1926-1996), our baby sister, was affectionately known as "Irene the Village Queen." She had deep brown eyes and black curly hair. She could do almost anything. She and I were kindred spirits and good friends. We shared secrets throughout our lives. We also shared clothes and hair curlers. Because we had only one set, she used them in the early evening and, before I went to bed, she had to surrender the curlers to me. Irene suffered terribly with painful rheumatoid arthritis. We miss Irene and John very much.

It has been said that life is like a road well traveled with many risks. Many have traveled it before me and many will travel it after me.

Those who have taken that road leave many lasting lessons we can glean from.

In my own personal life, my dear sister who died last year left a legacy of the example of hope and a positive life. She struggled with the pain of crippling rheumatoid arthritis and chronic bronchiectasis, a disease of the bronchial tubes, which compromised her breathing, necessitating the use of twenty-four-hour oxygen. Her husband of fifty years displayed true endless love for her as he cared for her every need. Together they kept a positive faith in God and in each other and always encouraged others, family and strangers.

There were many roadblocks with emergencies and surgeries. Her husband is a distance runner, who ran at early dawn while she was resting with the aid of oxygen. I suspect it was part of God's plan to keep his seventy-four-year-old body well so he could be there to care for her.

Life continues to be a risky road, but I believe it is worth the risk. Because each day is a new beginning, the road does rise up and meet us even as we plan the trip. We need guidance and hope with no guarantee. Regardless, prayerful life and love are worth the risk.

Mrs. Ruth Schlesser

"We are so grateful for these long-standing 'ties that bind.'"

From the time I was a little child, my mother read to me frequently — mainly Bible stories from the Old and New Testaments. When I grew a little older, I attended Sunday school faithfully each week and heard again many of the same stories told by dedicated, caring Sunday school teachers, pastors, and youth leaders.

My dad and mother and I attended the church as a family. When I learned to play the piano, I was able to play for Sunday school and church services and later for the choir, using the piano and finally a newly installed organ.

This inner-city church has seen a number of pastors and members come and go, and many other changes have taken place. However, long-ago members and friends still keep in touch and get together from time to time. We are so grateful for these long-standing "ties that bind."

Would you believe, at age seventy-one, I am still there — praising, praying, and playing — thanks be to God!

Mrs. Leila Hayes

"My life has been a combination of joy and sorrow,
but the joys have far outnumbered the latter."

Life is a journey. It is up to us to make the most of it. We have all the wonderful things God gave us — the sky, the earth, and the seas that surround us. All we have to do is live our lives as if every day is the last.

There are ups and downs along the way, but we accept them and go on. We become aware of others, our brothers and sisters regardless of race or creed.

My life has been a combination of joy and sorrow, but the joys have far outnumbered the latter. In my ninety-six years, I have lived to see many wonderful inventions and great progress in medical science. I am thankful to God for everything.

Mr. Don Boughner

*"My belief in God's caring hand in all things has been
a strength to me and will continue to be that for which
I daily give thanks."*

On my faith journey through life, as a child, son, college student, church member, soldier in the Army in Korea, friend, neighbor, and teacher, I have observed the universality of good and evil. My mother was a friend to all she knew and was always there when her care was needed. It has been my good fortune to have had good examples in my life, whether they attended church as I did or not. My belief in God's caring hand in all things has been a strength to me and will continue to be that for which I daily give thanks. Therefore, I feel the need daily also to reach out to someone with a hurt or need, and to let them know by word or deed that I care for them, giving help or encouragement, as I am able.

Mrs. Lorene Temple

*"We always end our day by making music, singing,
and giving thanks to God."*

I believe my outlook on life was formed from both my Christian faith and my early years of life. I was born in Louisiana to parents who were very poor sharecroppers. I learned to work at an early age in the fields picking cotton. My mother died in 1929 at the age of twenty-six. I was almost seven years old, my sister four years, and my little brother lacked five days of being one year old.

Our paternal grandparents took us in and, from her bed, my grandmother taught me how to cook. She was ill with cancer. When you have to grow up at the age of seven, you learn a lot very quickly. Anything anyone did for us was a great treat, like giving us food or hand-me-down clothes. You quickly learn the value of food and having a few clothes, and are also thankful to God for taking care of your needs.

I will always remember how I enjoyed the foods of two special people — one was my maternal grandmother. We always looked forward to going to her home and spending the night. She could not take care of us when my mother died because five of her nine children were still at home. My grandmother could make the best hot oatmeal in the world. There wasn't any "quick" or "instant" in those days. She would make a big pot of oatmeal and we would all line up on the wooden benches on each side of the long, crude, homemade table. She would dish us our oatmeal and we would put sugar and whole milk on it. Our milk at home was skimmed because we had to have the cream to churn in a hand crock for a little butter. To this day I dislike skimmed milk.

The other person was Aunt Mary. She lived about halfway between our house and where we walked three miles each way to school. She would see us coming home from school and, in the winter when we were very cold, she would call us in and give us homemade sugar cookies and butter. Her butter was the prettiest I have ever seen. It was very yellow and she would mold it in a wooden butter-mold press, and it would have a beautiful rose imprinted on top. Until she died, when I went back to my home in the South, I would visit Aunt Mary. We really loved each other.

When you have to move as much as sharecroppers (I counted twenty-one times), it is very hard in school. We moved just as my grade was about to start to learn fractions. Arithmetic was one of my favorite subjects. When I went to the new school, they were already into fractions and, because I didn't get the basics at the beginning, I was having a terrible time and was in tears. We, however, had a neighbor who was a well-educated man. One day I asked him if he knew how to do fractions. This blessed man came to teach me, and when he left I was so happy because he had taught me how to do fractions. This opened me up like sunshine. Needless to say, I didn't have any more problems with fractions and, to this day, I am eternally grateful to this man.

We had good schoolteachers. Our teachers were treated with respect, and it was an honor to be a teacher in those days. I believe if there were more love and respect in our world, it would be a much better place in which to live.

My outlook on life is reflected in my own family life. We are a closely knit family. A family reunion is held every Labor Day weekend, and thirty-five or forty of us celebrate Thanksgiving, Christmas, and the New Year together. We love each other and there is no backbiting.

We always end our day by making music, singing, and giving thanks to God. Our children have grown up in this tradition and I pray they will continue after we are gone. I firmly believe the family is the backbone of our nation and our world.

I think from this little writing you can tell I love life and the Master Craftsman who gave it to me. Each new day is a challenge and it's up to us to do our best.

Mrs. Lorene Temple and daughter Carol, Mother's Day, 1988

Mrs. Dorothy McInerney

*"The one thought that continually remains with me
is that you should always have faith in God
and believe in the power of prayer."*

I am eighty-one years old, have five children and six grandchildren. I met my husband-to-be in the spring of 1941. Bernard was in the Army at that time, so we didn't date too often. In October 1941, he was released from the Army because he was over the age of twenty-eight. However, he was ordered back into the service on February 7, 1942. Two months later, he was on a troop ship to Iceland for training. For thirty-nine months, our only means of communication was via the mail. This is when he was in the European Theatre. Most of our letters, I believe, got through the German blockade because the ships sailed in convoys. When the war in Europe ended, he returned quickly because he had so many "points" to his credit. We were married for over fifty years.

In my lifetime, I have been privileged to know two people whose lives were personally affected by World War II and who have had an impact on my life. One was a French woman. She was imprisoned because her husband was very active in the French Resistance. Her eldest son, Jean, who was about eighteen at the time, also left home and joined a group of underground Resistance. He killed a German officer

Bernard and Dorothy McInerney
with first child, 1946

and escaped, but the Germans found out. This boy eventually linked up with the U.S. Army and was attached to my fiancé's unit. He was killed at Dornot (outside Metz). My fiancé wrote to the family and told them all the facts he could regarding Jean's death. That is how we eventually became acquainted with his mother. The SS troops of the German Army came to her summer home outside of Paris and arrested her. She was taken away and sent to a work camp. In the meantime, her husband was also arrested and died of hunger in Buchenwald. She learned about her husband's and her son's deaths when she returned to Paris at the end of the war.

The other person was a Roman Catholic priest of the Byzantine Rite. He was Romanian, married, with two daughters. He was forced to leave his country alone. He and his wife were separated for seventeen years. She eventually was allowed to join him in the United States. He hadn't seen his daughters for many years. They both had married, and he had two grandchildren he had never seen. These people never lost faith and managed to survive and live useful lives.

The two families I mentioned, and their experiences during the war and after, enabled me to have a personal relationship with people who had actually suffered both physically and emotionally because of the war. Every morning I would read the paper and learn the latest news regarding the progress of the war, but it was impersonal. Knowing these two families brought me closer to the realities. Instead of reading about them, I actually could talk to them and learn about their experiences firsthand. It also made me realize how fortunate I was. Although this was a terrible experience for all of us who had loved ones in action, it seemed to me that it was not a time for self-pity because there were ten million men and women from the U.S. who were in the service, so no one was unique.

The one thought that continually remains with me is that you should always have faith in God and believe in the power of prayer. I try to do this and many good things have happened in my life. I have survived cancer for almost twelve years. My family is very close and we keep in touch constantly. We enjoy one another!

Father John Canavan

*"My legacy is simple. I want to be remembered as a very
human person who held onto his dreams and goals.
Also, a person who has reached out to touch the lives
of others with gentle love."*

I was born in late December 1926. My parents experienced the joys
and the trials of raising me and my sister along with my two brothers. The love they had for each other and their role as parents were
tested during the years of the Great Depression.

The marriage of my parents took place in St. Peter and Paul's
Church, County Armagh, Northern Ireland. Dad was a Protestant and
mother a Catholic. This marriage presented no bitterness between
them. Dad became a Catholic and was faithful in his religious responsibilities. He set a good example to his children. Often he entertained
us by singing hymns from his early childhood. Later, on my journey as
a parish priest, the ecumenical attitude that I was taught motivated me
to help bring some harmony between Catholics and Christians of
other persuasions.

My sister, Marie, after graduating from junior high school, took a
trip to Ireland with our mother. They were both thrilled with the visit.
The anticipation of their arrival helped to diminish the fears of the
seven-day boat trip. They also experienced the joy with relatives and
friends. However, a sudden, unexpected illness brought death to my

sister. The cause of death was diabetes. Mother's trip back to the States was filled with deep sorrow and grief. I was too young at age ten to feel empathy toward my mother. This tragedy left me without a sister — a sister who would have been extremely helpful to me in my priesthood. A beautiful framed picture of my sister hangs on the wall of my cottage/retirement home, which is an ever-present reminder of a special person in my family.

Father John Canavan, 1997

My formal education came from the public schools in east Dearborn. A helping hand was extended to me with the invitation to attend Henry Ford Trade School. These were delightful days for me as I enjoyed working and learning the skills of the automotive profession. Apart from the education, I gained a deep appreciation of the teachers. They treated me and the other students as their sons. In my reflection later in life, I realized that it was my duty to give back a portion of myself as I had been blessed by others.

After graduation in January 1945, I was drafted into the service. I volunteered for the paratroopers after basic training. Later, I was assigned as a chaplain's assistant. In admiration of the good done by the chaplain, I was motivated to pursue a call to life in the priesthood. My mother was delighted to hear of my decision to go to the seminary. College life was a big challenge for me. But with perseverance, prayers and faithful work, I was able to be ordained a priest of the Diocese of Detroit in June 1955. As a parish priest over these past forty-four years, I have touched the lives of countless thousands of people. Apart from the diversity in race, color, culture, and creed, we all share so

much in common. We are all pilgrim people. They have taught me a
great deal of the realities of life — the joys, the hopes, the needs, the
challenges and, especially, the pain of our struggles.

My assignment in the Diocese began at St. John's Church in
Monroe. After one year at the parish, I was sent to St. Joseph's Parish
in Erie to work among the Hispanic migrants. The following parishes
that I served, after a period of sickness due to migraine headaches,
were: St. Lawrence in Utica, St. Syril in Taylor, St. Basil in Eastpointe,
and then pastor of St. Constance Church in Taylor. As pastor of the
parish for twenty-seven years, I fulfilled my duties to the best of my
abilities. The guidelines of Vatican II, which opened the doors and
windows of the Church, gave me the encouragement to help imple-
ment the teachings of Catholicism. This effort helped bring about a
further sign of our Lord's presence to our community.

My housekeeper, Patricia, was a great blessing to me and to the
people of the parish. She never complained about her paralysis. She
was a person of living faith, a saintly person, and a wonderful friend.
She suffered a major stroke at the age of eighty-three. As her caregiver,
I experienced the challenge of doing whatever I was able to do to ease
her pain and suffering. One of the lessons I learned from the many visits to her nursing home is that caring for your loved one has a price.
The price was an expression of my love and deep appreciation for her.

In my journey as a parish priest, I sensed the formation and development of my personal value system. I believe that people want to be
loved, respected and accepted. I believe that people have been blessed
with many gifts and talents. People also have many needs and wants.
Perhaps my words and signs of affirmation have helped uplift those I
touched. I am also aware of my needs, especially friendship. I have
learned to be a giving person with unconditional love, and to give back
by showing my appreciation for what people have done for me is
something always on my mind.

My legacy is simple. I want to be remembered as a very human
person who held onto his dreams and goals. Also as a person who has
reached out to touch the lives of others with gentle love. As the
Israelites journeyed some forty years in the desert, seeking and longing

for God's love, so too I journey. I journey with a human heart to be nourished by others. I also journey, mindful of my stumbling disappointments, pains, and challenges, but with a song in my heart. I don't know where my journey will take me, but it is my journey.

Mrs. Cynthia Mayberry

*"Everyone stands back and watches as the ball drops
from the blue sky and lands securely into my left-handed
mitt. 'He's safe!' I hear one of my brothers shout
from home plate."*

There's a house on Hanlon Street in Westland, Michigan, where I grew up as the only girl in the midst of three brothers. My life was a happy one as I recall. I learned at an early age to play all sports left-handed even though I was born right-handed. There was no doubt this girl on the block was the only one who possessed a left-handed mitt for baseball. You see, my three brothers were all left-ies and, because of that, I learned at an early age the spirit of survival. Our parents are still married today after almost fifty years of being together. Our parents loved us kids, raised us with a value system, believed in discipline, took us to church, and believed in a hard day's work for an honest day's pay.

My father worked in a steel plant in Redford, Michigan, all of his working years. My mother went to work as a postal employee in Wayne, Michigan, when I was twelve.

My brothers and I attended public schools in Westland, which at that time was known as Nankin Township. We were a family who spent a lot of time together. We played games, hosted baseball games in our acre backyard, climbed huge oak trees, and visited our grandparents at least once a year because they lived out of state. We were basically a closely knit family who cared about the needs of each other. I can never remember in my entire childhood seeing alcohol or tobacco products in our home. I can never remember hearing my parents having an unkind word for one another.

Mrs. Cynthia Mayberry, age two, and her dad, Christmas Eve on Hanlon Street, Westland, Michigan, 1955

Many children grow up and take their "childhood scars" with them into adulthood, scars that they hide from others and even themselves. The scars I share with you are scars that came not from my childhood but later in life. When I reflect upon the scars of my life, I wonder at times if the reason mine are so visible is to remind me forever of where I received them and to teach me a lesson to never go there again. Each scar I will share with you has only made me a better, stronger, more alive individual. Each scar I bear has renewed my faith, rekindled my spirit, and restored my love for a God who never makes mistakes.

In 1971, I finished high school and decided to pursue an education in elementary teaching. After my undergraduate studies were complete, I began teaching second grade at the age of twenty-two. I instantly fell in love with teaching the first day I stood before children and began to challenge their minds to think and to always ask questions. There is nothing like teaching children to stretch themselves to levels they have never been to before. Watching a child learn how to put letters together to make sounds, then words, then to make sentences and on to paragraphs, and finally to create stories was incredible. Knowing that I had chosen a career with the opportunity to mold the lives of young people is as rewarding today as it was then.

After three years of teaching, I met a man who had custody of his three young children. In 1979 this was almost unheard of, and just the fact that he loved his children so much drew me instantly to him. We had a short courtship and in 1980 we were married, thus making me the instant mother of Johnathan who was seven, Jeremy who was six, and Valerie who was five. It was not an easy task to take on three small children then, nor would it be today. To walk into instant parenthood, one can only imagine the mistakes I made along the way. Mistakes that were never intentional, but nevertheless at the expense of all involved. I continued my teaching career as I searched to find my role as a parent literally overnight. There was a great deal of laughter, and many warm moments raising Johnathan, Jeremy, and Valerie. I have learned to keep those memories alive deep within my heart and many times use them to soothe the scars that were created along the way.

During the course of raising our three older children, we discovered that Johnathan was "profoundly deaf" and required medical attention during his entire growing years, including several surgeries, hearing aids, and on and on and on. Valerie, in her teen years, was diagnosed with scoliosis, which required an equal amount of medical attention, including back braces, doctor appointments, and so on. Although Jeremy suffered from no medical misfortunes, he missed his biological mother tremendously, thus bringing many years of discontentment and hurt.

A few years into our marriage, God blessed us with two beautiful children of our own, Christopher and Kathryn (Katie). For the first time in my life as a parent, I knew the depth of a love relationship between parent and child. I fell more in love with Chris and Katie each day. Both of our children had high medical needs. They required hundreds of doctor visits, hospital stays, transfusions, and endless hours of care. Blending our own children into an already-made family did not seem very hard at the time; however, the scars came later and still remain today.

In 1988, when I was thirty-four years old, raising five children, teaching school, and sailing through life at a hundred miles per hour, a storm came into my life that I was not prepared to deal with at all. It was a cold, blustery February afternoon as I drove to see a man by the name of Dr. Waldinger. The wind was whipping around the trees and, as it blew, one could feel the sting of Michigan winter in the air. The sun was shining bright; however, for some reason the sun did not hold the same warm affection in my soul as it had in previous days of my youth.

My mind began to reflect on all the days I had spent in the sun. Could anything that had given me so much physical pleasure at one time now be the cause for such immediate danger and concern? How could my previous years of an affair with the sun be the reason for this dreaded doctor appointment today? There is nothing in the entire world like the feeling of the hot sun baking down from the sky onto your bare skin. The sensation and warmth that the hot sun brings with it are incredible. As your bare skin welcomes the penetration of the sun's rays into its pores, you can sense the heat that radiates deep within your bones.

Again I questioned how a love affair with the sun could go bad. My mind began to wander back to my teen years, when I would lie afloat a ninety-nine-cent air mattress on a lake all day and bake my fair skin until it was so golden brown that my tan line would last easily until the Christmas season. And how about those college days and early into my teaching career, when I thought spring break was the highlight of each calendar year? I remembered one time in my early twenties when I was so sunburned during Easter break that, when I awoke the morning after a day at the beach, I fell down because my skin was so blistered I could not even stand.

How my mind was quickly brought back to the day's events as the warm sunshine was replaced by blowing snow and howling winds. My mission was very clear in my mind that day as I drove to see Dr. Waldinger. My mission was to get my husband and everyone else off my back. It seemed as though everyone in my family had become a doctor without a license to practice. Everyone was so concerned about this small, insignificant mole that had appeared on my inner right leg near my knee. How could such a small, dark mole have so many people in such great alarm?

The drive that day seemed like such a waste of time, not only for me but also for this doctor I had never met. My two small children were staying late in daycare so I could make this appointment. Our three older children were in different sporting events. Time was ticking away; the day was getting later and later. Dinner would not be on time because of this appointment, daycare would cost more, and on and on my thoughts went.

As I look back over almost eleven years since I first met Dr. Waldinger, I never would have thought a patient could grow to love and respect a physician as I have this man. It was Dr. Waldinger's diligence, intertwined with his compassion, that set him aside from all the rest. There was something very special about him that provided me with an instant trust in him. I sensed in Dr. Waldinger that he knew his limits as an earthly physician and left the rest up to our heavenly physician. He took one look at my leg and told me, point blank, that in his professional opinion I had a malignant melanoma that needed immediate attention. He proceeded to do a biopsy in his office that day. He sent me on my way and told me he would call me as soon as he had heard something.

Less than one week went by and the phone call came. Indeed, it was this same man I had only met one week earlier, and with his voice came that dreaded news. My biopsy had come back; it was certain I had a malignant melanoma. A wide margin removal was my only option at this point. Knowing very little about melanoma, but knowing enough to know that this type of cancer is a most aggressive killer, I decided not to argue. The appointment was made at the University of Michigan in Ann Arbor, Michigan, and that was that.

Suddenly I felt as though my life were not mine to make decisions for any longer. I hung up the phone that day with a mind that was racing to find the answers to all the questions I had. My thoughts were incredible. How could someone like myself who had never smoked or drank, someone who had gone to church all her life, be dealt such a harsh diagnosis like cancer? I had five children yet to raise. My baby was only two and was just coming out of her own major medical problems. I was in the prime of my life and way too busy to stop and deal with all that was happening to me.

Then I began to feel a deep loss, as though something had been taken away from me before I was ready to let go, or without my permission. I began to feel guilty and wonder if some sin in my life prior to this disease is what gave me this cancer. Perhaps the doctor was wrong. Perhaps I did not have cancer. Maybe they had me mixed up with some other woman. The questions kept coming, never stopping, never giving me the chance to collect my thoughts or even develop a plan of action. I went from anger to denial to depression. I can remember asking God to allow me enough days to see my children grow up. Now I ask God to allow me enough days to see my grandchildren grow up. The asking of God never stops, for there is no good time to say goodbye to the people you love.

Within a week I was at the University of Michigan in Ann Arbor being prepped for surgery, and another scar was placed on my body. This one was very visible and a constant reminder of my carefree days in the sun. I found in order for me to stay out of the sun I had to ask God to take away the love and passion that I had once had for the sun. I began to ask God to help me fall more in love with His Son rather than the sun I had so foolishly worshipped in past years.

Each day began to look different for me. I wanted to live my life to the fullest, because the more I read about melanoma, the more I began to realize how blessed I was that God had for some reason spared my life. There was an overwhelming desire to kill the cancer instead of allowing the cancer to kill me.

My children and the little things they did became much more precious to me. I began to take the extra time needed to listen and play, care and nurture. I held my children in my lap for hours at a time. I never minded and still don't when my children wake me in the wee hours of the night for comfort. I hug my children every day and tell them how much I love them and what they mean to me. Fixing special meals is not a burden to me but instead a delight. Some say I have spoiled my children over the years. I choose to say I have loved them as much as I can, realizing just how precious is each day I have with them.

My teaching career took on a more powerful attitude because I wasn't so sure at that time just what was happening to my life. My desire to continue my education became paramount. I enrolled at Eastern Michigan University as a graduate student in the summer of 1991. Thirteen months later I had taken thirty-four graduate credits and received a Master's Degree in Educational Leadership. Motivated and driven I was for sure. The summer of 1992, I took Christopher and Katie by myself on a thirty-one-day, 7,500-mile road trip to the Grand Canyon and back. The power I felt was incredible. Every moment of every day had to be explored. People still accuse me of "packing in" way too many things in a twenty-four-hour period. Every minute of every day must be a celebration of life.

However, in my quest to do the things I wanted to do, my relationship with my husband began to dissolve. By the middle of 1994, my marriage had ended and with it came more scars — the real, visible kind, the kind nobody can hide. My life had not only lost the sunshine I once loved, but it had also lost the sunlight of my life.

For three years I searched for some sunshine in my life. There were times when I wanted nothing more than to fly to a warm climate, put on a bathing suit, take off my hat and sunglasses, wear no sunblock, and just allow the sun to take my life from me.

But those two precious children God spared my life to see raised are what kept me going. Their smiles would remind me each day that life is worth living. They would remind me each morning that I did have a reason to keep on going, in spite of the scars that life had brought my way.

I began to find sunshine within my inner soul for the first time in a long time. I began to realize that scars are not so bad after all. For you see, if a person can learn from the scars of life, hopefully they will never have the same scars twice.

I continued to look at my scars in a different light and after many hours, days, weeks, and even years, I finally allowed them to teach me lessons that I intend to keep deep within my heart for the rest of my living days. If it means that I deliberately look at my scars each day to remind me never to revisit places that created the scars to begin with, then that is what I'll do.

Scars have a remarkable way of healing deep wounds. In October 1997, my husband, Gary, and I were remarried. What a spiritual healing for both of us! We both had learned some valuable lessons from the scars of life. I had learned that God had spared my life from a physical disease called cancer, not to have me die a spiritual death. God had been so gracious, allowing me more days on this earth, and I was going through life acting as though it was my right. Life is such a precious gift, and each day we wake up and see the sunshine we should say, "Thank you, God."

When I needed a physical healing, it was the spiritual healing that came to me and granted me more days, weeks, months, even years to live. It was the spiritual healing that came to me and gave me a peace to accept what I could not ever change. It was the spiritual healing that allowed me to accept God's perfect plan for my life in having the experience of cancer. For had I not had this experience, I am certain that my heart would have never been tender enough to start over with my husband, the father of our children.

Cancer is not a bad thing — only if you let it become one. Yes, it takes lives without the permission of the ones it invades. Yes, it shortens years and events for people and the ones they love. But cancer is also something that you must embrace.

If you don't embrace the pain, you will never allow yourself to grow from the pain or the scars that cancer leaves. Cancer shows people how urgent each day is. It teaches people that life is too short to be angry and hateful toward their brothers and sisters. It teaches one to treat each new day with a level of respect for the one who gave you breath.

My mind wanders back to my childhood days and to our baseball field on Hanlon Street in Westland, Michigan. One of my brothers slams the ball right to me. I reach out my left-handed mitt to catch the fly ball, knowing it doesn't matter whether I am right- or left-handed.

What matters is that I have the courage to reach out my mitt and catch the ball. I call it, "It's mine. It's mine." Everyone stands back and watches as the ball drops from the blue sky and lands securely into my left-handed mitt. "He's safe!" I hear one of my brothers shout from home plate.

Thirty-five years later, does it matter if the person on third was out or safe? No. What matters is we stayed in the game and kept playing. It's kind of like life, don't you think?

Cancer and the scars it leaves will change your life forever if you keep your heart tender to the sunshine. Bask in the sunlight He has to offer you. Allow His rays to soak deep into your soul. Feel the warmth that only He can provide. Hold strong to the promises that He will never leave you or forsake you. Believe in miracles, and when you have experienced one, be ready to share it with someone else who needs to hear your story. Pray for courage to accept the things you cannot change. Stay in the game even if your mitt doesn't fit. And you and the people who love you the most will never be the same . . . ever again.

Part Six

A Tribute to John L. Ulrich, M.D.

I lift mine eyes to the hills,
From where does my help come?
My help comes from the Lord,
Maker of heaven and earth.

— Psalm 121:1-2

John L. Ulrich, M.D.
(1915 – 1997)

D r. John L. Ulrich, a most distinguished physician and remarkable human being, is the inspiration for this book.

A patient, Mr. Robert Dougherty, echoes my sentiments when he writes, "As I've journeyed through life, I have met many famous people both in and out of the sporting world. But the one person who left a lasting impression on me was Dr. John Ulrich. From our very first meeting, I realized I was in a room with a very special person — one devoted to his family and to his God. He deeply cared for his patients, and especially for me, as he always asked how my wife and children were doing. His last words to me at every visit were 'May God bless you and your family.'"

Because I do not have Dr. Ulrich's recorded philosophy, I am including a letter he wrote to Marcy and me, which offers a glimpse of the essence of this extraordinary person.

12-16-92

Dear Tom and Marcy –

Thank you so much for
your remembrances of
Christmas : the pens and
poinsettias have helped with
the "cheer" –; we will treasure
your kindness.

I am positive your precious
children are looking forward
to sharing your Florida
trip. Our hearts warm each
time their names are mentioned.
Please hug them for us.

We know the time of R & R
will be so good for you
both. Enjoy the pleasant
respites, life affords you,
while you can.
May almighty God touch
each of you with His
blessings of the spirit
as you travel and
stretch your souls.
                Love John & Marlee.

John L. Ulrich, M.D.

I Dance With The Wind

I miss you so
Never enough time
To let go
I miss you so.

A rainbow of lilies
White pines dance with the wind
Nature's beauty abounds
As your memory
As your memory
God is with me
God is with me.

I miss you so
Never enough time
To let go
I miss you so.

Radiance of divine light
Illumination of love
Creation of peace
As your memory
As your memory
God is with me
God is with me
I dance with the wind
I dance with the wind.

Your love permeates my being
I am now seeing
Myself more clearly

God is with me
God is with me
I dance with the wind
I dance with the wind.

A rainbow of lilies
Radiance of divine light
God is with me
God is with me.

— Thomas P. Waldinger

Part Seven

Stretch Our Souls

To finish the moment, to find the journey's end in every step of the road, to live the greatest number of good hours, is wisdom.

— Ralph Waldo Emerson

Nature's Tap Dance

Winter's whisper
You can hear
Winter whispers
I am there.

Snow falls gently
Trees become statues
Stretch our souls
Stretch our souls.

I feel your presence
We have never met
Warmth and love
A silhouette.

Winter's whisper
You can hear
Winter whispers
I am there
Stretch our souls
Stretch our souls.

Sky meets the ocean
Waves create music
Sunlight reflects on the water
A shimmering path
Nature's tap dance.

You are in Africa
I sit at home
Stretch our souls
Stretch our souls.

— Thomas P. Waldinger

Chimes Of Remembrance

I stand alone
On this cold autumn day
Trees almost barren
Sky completely gray
Feeling your love
Feeling your joy
Wind and leaves
Wind and leaves
Chimes of remembrance
Chimes of remembrance.

Deep inside yourself
There is a strength
I can hear you say
Above and beyond
My centerpiece
Always release
Feeling your love
Feeling your joy
Wind and leaves
Wind and leaves
Chimes of remembrance
Chimes of remembrance.

I stand alone
On this cold autumn day
Clouds covering the sky
An umbrella of love
Wind and leaves
Wind and leaves
Chimes of remembrance
Chimes of remembrance.

Deep inside yourself
There is a strength
That can be nurtured
By love and truth
Righteousness and peace
Wind and leaves
Wind and leaves
Chimes of remembrance
Chimes of remembrance.

— Thomas P. Waldinger

Rain Becomes Mist

You have been with me
Since I came into the world
Nourishing my soul
Listening to my thoughts
A gentle love
A gentle hand.

Struggling and searching
Wandering and seeking
In times of despair
You were there
Always there.

Joy and sorrow
Dreams and tears
Always today
Never tomorrow
You were there
Always there.

The years have passed
We hold each other
Our love is stronger
Rest on my shoulder.

Rain becomes mist
Clouds become sunsets
A gentle love
A gentle hand.

When I walk
I feel you beside me
Know you are guiding me
A gentle love
A gentle hand.

Reverence for life
Revelation of thought
Awareness of being
A gentle love
A gentle hand
Rain becomes mist
Clouds become sunsets
To be in the world
Not of the world.

— Thomas P. Waldinger

A Rainbow Around The Moon

The world is weeping
I am wishing
You were by my side again
Holding you
Like a rainbow around the moon
My heart to heaven
I love you
I love you.

When we were together
It was always summer
A warm, gentle breeze
The sun glistened on the leaves
A rainbow around the moon
Roses were in bloom
Rain became
Kisses upon kisses
Kisses upon kisses.

The world is weeping
My heart to heaven
My eyes downward
From a single source
One human soul
The breath of early light
The sun glistens on the leaves
The breath of prayer
A rainbow around the moon
From a single source
One human soul.

The world is weeping
My heart to heaven
My eyes downward
The breath of early light
The breath of prayer
One human soul
One human soul
The world is weeping
I am wishing
You were by my side again
Holding you
Like a rainbow around the moon
My heart to heaven
I love you
I love you.

— Thomas P. Waldinger

Beautiful Soul

To enlighten and dream
To see beauty
In our differences
To inspire greatness
To search and search
And search again
Beautiful soul
Beautiful soul.

To never relinquish
Your wish
For justice
To never cease
Your pursuit
For truth
To search and search
And search again
Remember your spirit
Beautiful soul
Beautiful soul.

May the winter wind resonate
That your strength
Is found in love
May the warmth of the sun
Replenish your essence
May the changing moon
Encourage you each day
To search and search
And search again
Remember your spirit

Beautiful soul
Beautiful soul.

Over time
You have overcome
Know you are loved
The struggle has meaning
You are just beginning
To enlighten and dream
To inspire and discover
Remember your spirit
Remember your spirit
Know you are loved
Know you are loved
Beautiful soul
Beautiful soul.

— Thomas P. Waldinger

Fly Forever

Butterfly in the sun
Spread your wings
Fly forever
Fly for those
No longer here
Fly forever.

Rushing river
Silent stream
Calm the souls
Of those
Who remain
Who remain.

Pray for peace
The strength to bear
Pray for courage
The will to care.

Butterfly in the sun
Spread your wings
Fly forever
Fly for those
No longer here
Fly forever.

Lay aside every weight
Run the race
That is set before us
With humility and grace.

Rushing river
Silent stream
Calm the souls
Of those
Who remain
Who remain.

Butterfly in the sun
Rushing river
Silent stream
Bless the child
Who remains
Bless the child
Bless the child
Fly forever
Fly forever.

— Thomas P. Waldinger

A Dream Come True

Your face in my hands
Your voice in my soul
Your heart and mine
Entwined
Our world, our world.

Art in the sand
Hands create words
Your voice in my soul
Your heart and mine
Entwined
Our world, our world.

A place and time
So long ago
In my mind
It's yesterday.

Your face in my hands
Your voice in my soul
Your heart and mine
Entwined
Our world, our world.

Love and laughter
Joy and hope
Your gift to me
Always my love
My love always
My love, my love.

Love and laughter
Joy and hope
Your gift to me
My being, my thought
Bless your heart
Bless your heart.

Your face in my hands
Your voice in my soul
Your heart and mine
Entwined
Our world, our world.

At the final curtain
This is for certain
A dream come true
With you in my life
Always my love
My love always
My love, my love.

Your face in my hands
Your voice in my soul
Your heart and mine
Entwined
Our world, our world.

— Thomas P. Waldinger

Together Again

Tell me a story
Sing me to sleep
Hold me closely
Never let me go.

"Let the trees in the woods sing
Bless you and protect you
Be gracious to you
And give you peace."

We walked in the park
Winter wind was swirling
Snow crunched in the dark
Leaves were crisp.

Rushing streams of spring
Leaves were soft
Our hands together
Mine was smaller
I remember, I remember.

"Let the trees in the woods sing
Bless you and protect you
Be gracious to you
And give you peace."

All over the world
So many places
So many faces
Coming home to my friend
Together again

Coming home
Coming home.

Tell me a story
Sing me to sleep
Hold me closely
Never let me go.

— Thomas P. Waldinger

I Begin As I End

Wonder of creation
Joy of love
Search for wisdom
Because of you
My faith renewed
My soul imbued
With love and hope.

My salvation
True inspiration
Because of you
My faith renewed
My soul imbued
With love and hope.

Now I know
What life was teaching me
It's a lovely gift
True inspiration
My salvation
Stretch our souls
Stretch our souls.

In your presence
A healing of the heart
Your spiritual essence
Beloved and precious
Stretch our souls
Stretch our souls.

I begin
As I end
Because of you
My faith renewed
My soul imbued
With love and hope
True inspiration
My salvation
Stretch our souls
Stretch our souls.

— Thomas P. Waldinger

About the Author

Thomas P. Waldinger, M.D., is a board certified dermatologist in private practice in Dearborn, Michigan. He specializes in geriatric dermatology and skin cancer.

Dr. Waldinger received a Bachelor of Science Degree with High Distinction from the University of Michigan. He is a graduate of the University of Michigan Medical School. His post-graduate training was also completed at the University of Michigan in the Department of Family Practice and the Department of Dermatology.

Dr. Waldinger is the author of two previous books, *The Wisdom of Life Through My Patients* and *Stretch Our Souls*, and is author or co-author of eleven peer-reviewed publications in the field of dermatology. His honors include graduating Phi Beta Kappa from the University of Michigan and recognition in *The Best Doctors in America*® and *Best Doctors.*® Dr. Waldinger and his wife Marcy live in Ann Arbor, Michigan.

Index of Poems, Stories, and Letters